PARADOX AND TRUTH

PARADOX AND TRUTH

RETHINKING VAN TIL ON THE TRINITY BY
COMPARING VAN TIL, PLANTINGA, AND KUYPER

Ralph A. Smith

CANON PRESS ■ Moscow, Idaho

Ralph A. Smith, *Paradox and Truth: Rethinking Van Til on the Trinity by Comparing Van Til, Plantinga, and Kuyper*
Second edition, updated and revised
© 2002 by Ralph A. Smith

Published by Canon Press, P.O. Box 8729, Moscow, ID 83843
800-488-2034 / www.canonpress.org
Printed in the United States of America.
Cover design by Paige Atwood

03 04 05 06 07 08   9 8 7 6 5 4 3 2 1

Thanks to SIL International for freely distributing the Greek and Hebrew fonts used in this book.

Library of Congress Cataloging-in-Publication Data

Smith, Ralph Allan.
    Paradox and truth : rethinking Van Til on the trinity by comparing Van Til, Plantinga, and Kuyper / Ralph A. Smith.
    p. cm.
  Includes bibliographical references and index.
    ISBN 1-59128-002-8 (pbk.)
 1. Trinity. I. Title.
    BT111.3 .S65 2002
    231'.044—dc21   2002012046

This book is dedicated to Frank, a Christian businessman who has generously and faithfully supported the ministry of our research center for over ten years. Frank's kindness is all the more remarkable in that he does not entirely agree with our theological position. On the doctrine of the Trinity and its importance for the Christian life, however, I am sure he fully concurs. Without his support this book would hardly have been possible.

Contents

Acknowledgments

It is a blessing to be able to thank others for the help they have given, so I am glad that for the second edition of this book, I have the opportunity to add to the list of those to whom I may express my gratitude.

For the first edition of this book, I acknowledged my indebtedness to James Jordan, not only for the fact that his books and Biblical Horizons newsletters stimulated my thinking about the Trinity, but also for the counsel and instruction that he provided through email. I also mentioned the Rev. Jeffrey J. Meyers, who has introduced me to a wide variety of books on the Trinity and has given encouragement and assistance through email for years.

Now, for this edition, I also wish to thank Doug Jones, who suggested the possibility of the book coming out in a Canon Press edition, and Peter Leithart, who offered both encouragement and helpful criticism, especially in chapter 4. Peter's comments made the chapter much better than it would have been. My own children helped this time as well. My son Ben Zedek offered numerous suggestions and pointed out misprints. My daughter Emeth corrected further minor problems and put the book into proper digital form for me.

Once again I am also happy to express my appreciation for the support of the Church of Christian Liberty in the United States and for the help of our own church here in Japan, the Mitaka Evangelical Church.

Introduction

Cornelius Van Til's doctrine of the Trinity has been variously viewed. On the one hand, some have misconstrued it as heretical or attacked it as rash and dangerous. On the other hand, a not insignificant group of theologians and Christian writers has found Van Til's doctrine of the Trinity to be a fruitful source for serious work to develop a truly Christian worldview. The contrast between the two groups' evaluation of Van Til could not be greater. Evaluating Van Til is something of a theological problem, which has now become further complicated by recent studies of the doctrine of the Trinity critical of Augustine's formulation—the foundation of Van Til's approach. A Reformed representative of those critical of Augustine is Cornelius Plantinga, Jr.[1] who offers, in the place of the traditional statements of the doctrine, a social view of the Trinity.

This recent study of the Trinity invites reconsideration of Van Til's view. Does Plantinga's social view of the Trinity and recent critique of Augustine require a revision of Van Til's approach? What about Van Til's use of nontraditional language? Is it legitimate or is it a "novelty" that causes confusion? What are the worldview implications of Van Til's view of the Trinity

[1] Cornelius Plantinga, Jr., "The Threeness/Oneness Problem of the Trinity," *Calvin Theological Journal* 23 (no. 1, April 1988): 38. Hereafter referred to as "TOPT."

and does Plantinga's view significantly alter these? To consider these and similar questions, we introduce and evaluate Cornelius Plantinga's social view of the Trinity, briefly explain and attempt to defend certain aspects of Van Til's view, comparing it with Plantinga's, and, finally, suggest a revision of Van Til's view that sets the doctrine of the Trinity more clearly at the center of systematic and biblical theology and the Christian worldview. It is my purpose to help bring Van Til's profound exposition of the Trinity back into the discussion of this doctrine and, in that connection, to help stimulate further consideration of the worldview implications of the doctrine of the Trinity.

The Relative Neglect of Van Til

One reason for this paper is the relative neglect of Van Til by evangelicals. Considering the literature produced by his followers, one would think that even theologians who did not favor Van Til's views would have much to say about him, but this is not the case. Evangelical theologian Stanley Grenz, for example, who has recently written a systematic theology centered in the doctrine of the Trinity,[2] writes as if not only Van Til but even John Calvin—who provided the most sententious discussion of the Trinity in the entire Reformation era[3]—did not exist. Karl Barth, Karl Rahner, Jurgen Moltmann, and Wolfhart Pannenberg[4] are, for Grenz, the twentieth century theologians who have made contributions which deserve our attention, not Van Til. The leading evangelical

---

[2] Stanley J. Grenz, *Theology for the Community of God* (Nashville: Broadman and Holman, 1994). Grenz is an exception to the evangelical trend to neglect the Trinity, but by ignoring Calvin and Van Til, he has limited his ability to apply it broadly.

[3] See the famous essay by B. B. Warfield, "Calvin's Doctrine of the Trinity," in his *Calvin and Augustine* (Philadelphia: Presbyterian and Reformed, 1956).

[4] Grenz studied under Pannenberg.

theologian of the second half of the century, Carl F. H. Henry, writing in 1982, when Van Tillians were in the process of publishing a rapidly growing body of literature which related the Trinity to academic and everyday life, went so far as to say:

> Louis Berkhof, Cornelius Van Til, J. Oliver Buswell, Jr., Gordon H. Clark, and Samuel Mikolaski support the orthodox view in their theological writings. But American evangelical theology has not on the whole contributed significant literature to the current revival of trinitarian interest.[5]

Was Henry ignorant of the fact that Van Til taught the doctrine of the Trinity as the biblical solution to the problem of the one and the many and therefore as relevant to every academic or philosophical problem? What could be more significant than a view of the Trinity which places the doctrine not only in the center of the entire theological enterprise, but also every academic and practical discipline, a view of the Trinity which sets forth the triune God as the very heart of the entire Christian worldview?

Van Til may or may not have succeeded, but he attempted nothing less. His view deserves attention, and those who decide that he did not succeed have the opportunity to take up the challenge to offer a better approach. For whether or not Van Til was correct in the way he expounded the doctrine of the Trinity and its place in the Christian worldview, can any Christian doubt that God Himself, as the triune Creator, Redeemer, and Lord of all, must be the foundation, the center, and the aim of all Christian thought?

---

[5] Carl F. H. Henry, "God Who Stands and Stays, Part One," *God, Revelation and Authority* (Waco, Tex.: Word, 1982), 5:212.

The Evangelical Worldview and the Trinity

Contrary to what one might expect, among evangelical Christians the doctrine of the Trinity seems not to be considered an important part of the Christian worldview—if, that is, we are to judge their faith by the place the doctrine of the Trinity holds in published studies of the Christian worldview. A brief survey of some of the major evangelical writers suggests that the Trinity is secondary at best. Francis Schaeffer, a student of Van Til and the evangelical writer who popularized the idea of the "Christian worldview," did give attention to the Trinity,[6] but unlike Van Til, Schaeffer did not make the doctrine of the Trinity a central concern. Other evangelical writers on the Christian worldview, though following Schaeffer in their concern to relate and contrast Christianity with other religions and philosophies in the broad strokes of a worldview approach, either did not catch Schaeffer's emphasis on the Trinity or decided not to follow it.

To cite only a few examples, James W. Sire's otherwise excellent book *The Universe Next Door* mentions the doctrine of the Trinity in passing, but the doctrine plays no important part at all in his discussion, apart from a brief mention in which Sire emphasizes that the Trinity demonstrates the Christian worldview is personal.[7] Ronald H. Nash's reference to the Trinity is no doubt intended to communicate to the reader that he considers it essential to the Christian position, but once mentioned, the doctrine of the Trinity is no longer

[6] For example, Schaeffer writes, "Every once and a while in my discussions someone asks how I can believe in the Trinity. My answer is always the same. I would still be an agnostic if there were no Trinity, because there would be no answers. Without the high order of personal unity and diversity as given in the Trinity, there are no answers" (*He Is There and He Is Not Silent* [Wheaton, Ill.: Tyndale House, 1972], 14).

[7] James W. Sire, *The Universe Next Door: A Basic Worldview Catalog* (Downers Grove, Ill.: InterVarsity, 1976), 24–25.

important in the argument.[8] Nash's "touchstone proposition"—the proposition that expresses the fundamental truth of reality in his worldview—is: "Human beings and the universe in which they reside are the creation of the God who has revealed Himself in Scripture."[9] Now the God of the Bible is certainly the triune God. But if the fact of God's triunity is essential to our worldview, that fact needs to be demonstrated and then expounded so that Christians can see what the doctrine of the Trinity means for Christian thought and life. Nash makes no attempt to do this. Neither does R. C. Sproul in his *Lifeviews: Understanding the Ideas that Shape Society Today.*

The list of evangelical authors who either ignore the doctrine of the Trinity or treat it only in passing could be extended.[10] Thus, what Karl Rahner wrote of Catholics applies almost equally to evangelicals:

> We must be willing to admit that, should the doctrine of the Trinity have to be dropped as false, the major part of religious literature could well remain virtually unchanged.[11]

The words of Jurgen Moltmann are also appropriate:

> Why are most Christians in the West, whether they be Catholics or Protestants, really only 'monotheists' where the experience and practice of their faith is concerned? Whether God is one or triune evidently makes as little difference to

[8] Ronald H. Nash, *Worldviews in Conflict: Choosing Christianity in a World of Ideas* (Grand Rapids: Zondervan, 1992), 35.

[9] Ibid., 52.

[10] Even Gary DeMar, a Van Tillian, does not do justice to the centrality of the Trinity in what is one of the best short introductions to the Christian worldview, *War of the Worldviews: A Christian Defense Manual* (Atlanta: American Vision, 1994).

[11] Karl Rahner, *The Trinity*, trans. Joseph Donceel, with new introduction by Catherine Mowry Lacugna (1970; reprint, New York: Crossroad, 1997), 10–11.

the doctrine of faith as it does to ethics. Consequently the doctrine of the Trinity hardly occurs at all in modern apologetic writings which aim to bring the Christian faith home to the modern world again. Even new approaches made by fundamental theology do not begin with the Trinity.[12]

Van Til stands in utter contrast to this tendency. He has not only asserted that the doctrine of the Trinity is important, but has also shown how it relates to other academic disciplines and to the history of theological and philosophical thought. He challenges both traditional thinking about the problem of the one and the many and traditional logic. His view that the Bible itself must be the standard for all human thought is a correlate of his view of the Trinity. Finally, Van Til's doctrine of the Trinity is grounded in the Christian doctrine of worship as well as the doctrine of salvation. With slight revision, Van Til's approach to the doctrine of the Trinity promises to advance the whole idea of distinctly Christian thought.

[12] Jurgen Moltmann, *The Trinity and the Kingdom* (Minneapolis: Fortress Press, 1981), 1. Moltmann, of course, had a different audience in mind.

Chapter One
Plantinga's View of the Trinity

In a now famous article, "The Threeness/Oneness Problem of the Trinity," Cornelius Plantinga Jr. addresses what he considers a "central conceptual problem" in the doctrine of the Trinity, a doctrine that "bristles with problems and questions."[1] According to Plantinga, this central problem "dwarfs" all other problems connected with the Trinity.[2] Furthermore, one's solution to this problem contains profound implications for one's formulation of other doctrines. For, as Plantinga points out at the very beginning of his article, Christian doctrines come in "conceptual clusters" with the result that how one conceives of the doctrine of sin, for example, will more or less determine how one must view the doctrine of election. Although this notion applies to every doctrine, the doctrine of the Trinity is the supremely resonant doctrine—the central and distinguishing Christian affirmation about God without which Christianity as such cannot exist. Thus, few would disagree that "a particular or peculiar statement of the doctrine of the Trinity will, for the sake of coherence, compel adjustments in nearly all other doctrinal areas."[3]

---

[1] "TOPT," 38.
[2] Ibid., 38.
[3] Ibid., 37.

The Oneness/Threeness Problem

The central problem of the doctrine of the Trinity comes to expression in the "debate between Karl Barth and his followers on the one side and social trinitarians on the other." Plantinga defines the problem of the oneness and threeness of God in these terms: "Suppose the divine life includes both a three and a one. What are the referents of these numbers? Three what? And one what?"[4] Barth offered the controversial answer that God's threeness consisted in "modes of being." God's oneness for Barth may be said to be in His personhood. God is only one personality, which is His one active, speaking, divine Ego. The Father, Son, and Spirit are that one. Furthermore, according to Barth, if we should ascribe personhood, in the full modern sense of the term, to each of the three persons, we would have unmitigated tritheism.[5]

Contrary to Barth, Leonard Hodgson argued that the threeness question cannot be solved by reference to "modes" in God. The three are distinct persons "in the full sense of that word." Hodgson even used the language of three "intelligent, purposive centres of consciousness."[6] This is the social doctrine of the Trinity which views God as a society consisting of three truly distinct persons. In addition to the Barthian and social trinitarian views, Plantinga interacts with a third view, the traditional Catholic view, which, according to Plantinga, offers a paradoxical answer to the questions above.

[4] Ibid., 38.

[5] Ibid., 38–39. Plantinga discusses Barth's views in some detail in footnotes. He seems to be of the opinion that Barth's later writings do not significantly shift his view of the Trinity and that, when all else is said and done, it is not really unfair to describe Barth as a modalist. This is disputed among experts on Barth's theology, but, interestingly, Van Til also viewed Barth as a modalist. From my own reading that seems like a fair analysis, though one must admit that Barth is complex enough for there to be doubt.

[6] Ibid., 39.

To contrast the various views and explain the third answer, the problem is restated in terms of the modern concept of a person as "a self-conscious subject, a center of action, knowledge, love, and purpose." In those terms, Plantinga asks, "how many persons does God comprise?" The Barthian answer is that God is one person. The social trinitarians answer that God is three persons. The traditional Catholic answer is more complicated. "These trinitarians seem to want to answer the central question both ways. God comprises three persons in some full sense of 'person.' But since each of these is in fact identical with the one divine essence, or each is in fact a center of exactly the same divine consciousness, the *de facto* number of persons in God is finally hard to estimate."[7]

To aid our reflection on these three options, Plantinga suggests that we consider each of them through the summary verses of the Athanasian Creed:

(15) So the Father is God, the Son is God, and the Holy Spirit is God;

(16) And yet they are not (or there are not) three Gods, but one God.

The main section of Plantinga's article goes on to offer analogies that illustrate the three approaches to the doctrine of the Trinity, seeking to show how each approach fits with the Athanasian Creed.

THREE ANALOGIES OF THE TRINITY COMPARED

Plantinga wants to know what it is "like" to confess that the Father, Son, and Spirit are each God, but yet they are not three gods, but one God. He offers three analogies. First, Plantinga asks, "Is it like saying John Cooper is professor of

---

[7] Ibid., 40.

theology at Calvin Seminary, Henry Zwaanstra is professor of theology at Calvin Seminary, and Ted Minnema is professor of theology at Calvin Seminary, and yet they are not three Calvin professors, but only one?" This seems hardly appropriate. Plantinga suggests that on this view verse 15 of the Creed contradicts verse 16, adding, "Here one instinctively feels the point of the seventeenth-century antitrinitarian complaint that trinitarians simply do not know how to count."[8]

The second analogy offered is the following, "The oldest native Minnesotan teaching philosophy at Calvin College is Nick Wolterstorff; the author of *Until Justice and Peace Embrace* is Nick Wolterstorff; and the only Michigander who loves the music of Messiaen is Nick Wolterstorff; yet, there are not three Nick Wolterstorffs but only one." The problem with this analogy is that "translated into trinity doctrine, we have here an analogy not for biblical or even classical trinitarianism but rather for the heresy of modalism."[9] On this view, God is one person only and the three names simply distinguish three different functions or roles that God fulfills.

The third analogy comes from an old TV Western. "The Cartwright family includes a son Adam, who is tall, silent, and serious; a son Hoss who is massive, gap-toothed, indelicate; and a son Little Joe, who is a roguish and charming ladies' man." The three are one in that they are all said to be "family." Adam is family, Hoss is family, Little Joe is family. There are not three Cartwright families, but one.[10] The problem with this view is that it appears to suggest what would be called "tritheism"—three different gods who have decided to join the same club.

These three analogies set forth the main options: "a classically paradoxical position (there are three Calvin professors

---

[8] Ibid., 41.
[9] Ibid., 41.
[10] Ibid., 42.

and yet there is only one) that seems incoherent; a modalist heresy (one person, Nick Wolterstorff, who plays three roles); and what looks like a tritheist heresy (three Cartwrights who compose one Cartwright family)."[11] According to Plantinga,

> The situation looks doctrinally familiar: coherent views on either end of a spectrum are called heretical, while the middle view, trying to have it both ways, seems utterly paradoxical and literally unbelievable. People who take this middle position often construe the orthodox claim as holding that in God each of Father, Son, and Spirit is a distinct person; yet they aren't three persons but one. And in some quarters this view is dignified with the term 'mystery.' But, of course, without equivocation there's nothing really mysterious about the claim that in God there both are and aren't three persons. In fact it's not really a claim at all, for what it affirms it also denies. The middle way isn't a mystery but a mess, and it ought to be rejected.[12]

It is noteworthy that Plantinga's rhetorical finesse and zeal come to expression in opposition to the traditional orthodox view rather than Barth's modalism, though he does not judge the traditional view to be heretical, as he does Barth's doctrine. Be that as it may, after this introduction, Plantinga offers a closer look at the three options that includes some discussion of the history of the doctrine of the Trinity as well.

Plantinga on the Western Latin Option

The first view that Plantinga treats in more detail is the traditional view still defended by Catholics and many Protestants. "In a number of sources from Augustine through Boethius, the Fourth Lateran Council, and Thomas Aquinas to contemporary Catholic writers who are traditionalists—in this long line of sources we find the first option (what I call

[11] Ibid., 42–43.
[12] Ibid., 43.

the standard Western option) in all its glory. Augustine is pretty clearly its first significant proponent. In him and in his successors one finds classically paradoxical statements of trinitarian doctrine."[13] What Plantinga wants to know is exactly where this doctrine came from. He suggests that it is a composite doctrine put together from two disparate sources.

Augustine's first source is the Bible, especially the Gospel of John. Here Augustine finds and faithfully reproduces a doctrine of God in which there are three persons who each has "his own memory, intelligence, and will; or memory, understanding, and love." According to John, the three persons mutually know, love, and glorify one another. There are, in other words, three subjects in God, each with all of the faculties that we regard as essential to the possession of personhood. Plantinga concludes that, in so far as we view this aspect of his doctrine, "Augustine looks as much like a Johannine pluralist as his Greek contemporaries, the Cappadocians, and as Hilary did a generation earlier."[14]

Complications are introduced through the Neo-Platonic doctrine of simplicity, the other source of Augustine's doctrine of the Trinity. The special problem is the notion that God is a simple being so that "in God persons and attributes are identical, as are persons and the sum of the attributes, the divine essence."[15] Plantinga's analysis here is important:

> Thus, for Augustine the Father is great, the Son is great, and the Holy Spirit is great, and yet there are not three greatnesses (not *tres magnitudines*), nor three greats, nor even three who are great (not *tres magni*), but only one great thing (only *unum magnum*). In the Augustine/Neo-Platonic Trinity there is exactly one divine essence or

---

[13] Ibid., 43.
[14] Ibid., 45.
[15] Ibid., 45.

substance or nature. This divine essence, says Augustine, is 'the thing that God is.' God the Trinity is simple. God the Trinity is identical with the divine essence. In fact, in the Trinity each of Father, Son, and Spirit is identical with this one thing, with this one divine essence. No one is just an instance of it, or an exemplification of it, for then each would have greatness or other attributes only by participation and could not, therefore, be ultimately divine. Each of Father, Son, and Spirit is identical with greatness itself, or with the greatest possible thing. In Book 6 it turns out that each of the attributes— greatness, almightiness, holiness, and so on—is identical with all the others. In Book 7 Augustine rejects the whole apparatus of genus/species/individual in application to God. There aren't three species—Father, Son, and Spirit—of the one genus God, or three individuals— Father, Son, and Spirit—of the one species God, for whether conceived of as genus or species, God, or the essence of God, has exactly one instance. God the Trinity is the only instance of Godness, the essence of God. God the Trinity is moreover identical with Godness-itself, the only divine thing. And each of Father, Son and Spirit is identical with that thing. So Godness itself, the only divine thing, the Trinity, and each of Father, Son, and Spirit all turn out to be really the same thing.[16]

In Plantinga's opinion, Augustine's view is "heavily monist and Neo-Platonic." The emphasis on God's oneness is so strong that Harnack says Augustine "only gets beyond modalism by the mere assertion that he does not wish to be a modalist." Plantinga can only defend Augustine from this charge by the explanation that his position is contradictory: "As the examples from Book 15 show, Augustine does hold that there are three persons in God. But he also holds, even if

---

[16] Ibid., 45–46.

he doesn't say so, that there is only one such person. For if the Father, Son, and Spirit are all identical with the divine essence, if they are not just instances of it or particularized exemplification of it, then it follows that none is a person distinct from the other." What is regarded as Augustine's attempt to combine Neo-Platonic notions of divine simplicity and the biblical doctrine of God's triune personhood may be the tradition of the West, but it is judged to be profoundly unsuccessful.

Thomas Aquinas follows essentially the same approach. On the one hand, the persons of the Trinity are presented as real persons, just as they are in the Gospel of John. On the other hand, each person is regarded as the whole divine essence. The difference between the persons is found in the "relations," of which in classical doctrine there are four.[17] Paternity is the relation which defines the Father as the Father of the Son. Filiation defines the Son as the one who is begotten. Procession is the relation which constitutes the Spirit as Spirit. The fourth relation, spiration, also refers to the Spirit as the one who is "spirated" from the Father and Son. This establishes, or seems to establish, relative differences among the persons. But, in Plantinga's words, "Thomas simplifies things so aggressively that even that difference is eventually washed out. For each person is identical with his relation: the Father just is paternity; the Son just is filiation; the Spirit just is procession. Further, these relations themselves, Thomas explicitly says, are all really the same thing as the divine essence. They differ from it only in intelligibility, only in perception, only notionally, not ontologically. For everything in the universe that is not the divine essence is a creature."[18]

----

[17] Plantinga refers only to the three "person-constituting" relations—paternity, filiation, procession—but these are also classified as "relations of opposition" along with one more relation, spiration. In addition, the four relations of opposition are combined with unoriginatedness to become the five "notions."

[18] Ibid., 47.

For Plantinga, this position is "impossible to hold." As he explains, "The threeness part of it is biblical and plausible; the oneness part of it is both implausible and unbiblical, and is, in any case, inconsistent with the threeness part." What this means in terms of the Athanasian Creed is spelled out as follows: "The Father is the divine essence, the Son is the divine essence, and the Holy Spirit is the divine essence; yet there are not three divine essences but only one—the very thing that God the Trinity is." This statement may be analyzed in two ways, both of which fail to accomplish what the traditional view aims to accomplish: a biblically consistent statement of the doctrine of God. First, Plantinga suggests that if Father, Son, and Spirit are taken as mere names for the divine essence, then the conclusion is not inconsistent. But this is mere modalism. Second, if Father, Son, and Spirit are taken as names of persons, then the statement reduces persons to essences, which are abstract. Each person would be a set of properties and the three sets of properties would be identical. The persons themselves thus disappear.

All this does not mean that the classical doctrine cannot be stated so as to be meaningful and biblical. In fact, confessional statements of the doctrine may be read in a manner that seems to satisfy Plantinga, for these statements do not say "flat out that there are three divine persons and yet there aren't." They refer rather to three persons and one essence. "Provided you understand this essence generically (i.e., that it's the set of properties any person must have to be divine, and the set that, in fact, Father, Son, and Holy Spirit all do have), and provided you hold that Father, Son, and Spirit have it instead of being it, there is no difficulty whatever in holding that there are three persons but only one God—where God is a name for the generic essence."[19]

[19] Ibid., 48.

Plantinga on Barthian Modalism

Plantinga takes far less time with modalism, presumably because it is so obviously defective from a biblical point of view. What modalism has to offer is coherence. For the modalist, there is "one God but three modes of His being." This means that there is "in the divine life exactly one thinker, actor, lover, knower, covenant-maker; one person in any full sense of personhood; one center of love, act, and consciousness who is, however, perpetually existent, perennially existent, in three modes of his being."[20] The problem is not, as Plantinga concedes, with the word *mode* itself, for in spite of the abstract connotations of the term, one could speak of individual human persons as "modes of human being" so that *mode* is just a technical term for the particularization of human nature in the individual. But though this use of the word may be possible, it is not the meaning of modern modalists—among whom, according to Plantinga, are such well known names as Karl Barth, Eberhard Jungel, Hendrikus Berkhof, Robert Jenson, Karl Rahner, and Dorothy Sayers. Their views are, in a word, "reductionistic."

> They reduce three divine persons to modes or roles of one person, thus robbing the doctrine of God of its rich communitarian overtones. They often do this, incidentally, while trying simultaneously to harvest from trinity doctrine all the best fruits of a more social view, such as intratrinitarian harmony, mutuality, fellowship, and intersubjectivity. Nobody is more eloquent on these benefits than Karl Barth. Barth wants in heaven a model of covenant fellowship, the archetype of mutuality that we image as males and females, and a ground for the ethics of agape. But, to tell the truth, his theory cannot

[20] Ibid., 48–49.

consistently yield these fruits. For modes do not love at all. Hence, they cannot love each other.[21]

Thus "modalism is stuck with a pluralist image of God derived from a monist concept of God."[22] This is not only philosophically an impossible formulation, it is contrary to the biblical witness of God.

Plantinga on the Social View of God

Plantinga returns to his illustration about the Cartwright family with the intention of showing that it is not really tritheist and that equivocation on the word *family* is not really a problem. Plantinga explains, "This option amounts to a social view of the Trinity. According to this view, the holy Trinity is a transcendent society or community of three fully personal and fully divine entities: the Father, the Son, and the Holy Spirit or Paraclete. These three are wonderfully unified by their common divinity, by the possession by each of the whole divine essence—including, for instance, the properties of everlastingness and sublimely great knowledge, love, and glory." Each of the three persons on this view is distinct, but "scarcely an individual or separate person."[23]

The three persons are not, in this view, "three miscellaneous divine persons each of whom discovers he has the divine essence and all of whom therefore form an alliance to get on together and combine their loyalties and work." A view of this sort would certainly be tritheistic. It is not, however, tritheistic to view the Father, Son, and Spirit as distinct persons who not only share a common divine essence, but who also mutually indwell one another so perfectly and completely that we must say there is "in the divine life a

---

[21] Ibid., 49.
[22] Ibid., 50
[23] Ibid., 50.

mysterious, primordial in-ness or oneness relation that is
short of a oneness of person but much closer than mere
common membership in a class."[24] This is what biblical words
like *Father* and *Son* point to, for the Son has a relationship with
the Father so that the two persons "are of one substance not
only generically but also quasi-genetically. The Son is not only
equally divine with the Father; he is also the Father's Son; he
is, so to speak, his Father all over again. Father and Son are
not just members of the class of divine persons; they are also
members of the same family."[25]

What this means is defined carefully:

> Each of Father, Son, and Spirit possesses, then, the whole
> generic divine essence and a personal essence that distin-
> guishes that person from the other two. Both kinds of es-
> sence unify. The generic essence assures that each person
> is fully divine. The personal essences relate each to the
> other in unbroken, unbreakable love and loyalty. For the
> Father has essentially the property of being permanently
> related to the Son in an ineffable closeness akin to a par-
> ent/child relation. The Son has essentially the property
> of being permanently related to the Father in an ineffable
> closeness akin to a child/parent relation. Let us say that
> the Spirit has essentially the property of being the Father
> and Son's loyal agent. They in turn have the complement
> of this property: it is essential to them to have the Spirit
> as their loyal agent.[26]

On the social view, the Athanasian Creed affirms that the
Father is divine, the Son is divine, and the Spirit is divine, yet
there are not three Gods. On this social view, the denial of
tritheism has at least three possible interpretations, any or all

---

[24] Ibid., 51.
[25] Ibid., 51.
[26] Ibid., 52.

of which could be meant. First, the word *God* may be used, as it often is in the New Testament, as the special name of the Father, in which case, the Athanasian Creed affirms that there is only one fount of divinity, only one God in the way that the Father is God. Second, *God* may be used as the name for the divine essence. There are, then, three persons but one and only one generic Godhead or Godness, which each of the persons possesses. This accords with the traditional Latin interpretation of the Trinity, unless it is said that the three persons do not possess the divine nature but are each identical to it. Third, one could use *God* to designate the whole Trinity, as Augustine does. What this means is that "the Father is a divine person, the Son is a divine person, and the Holy Spirit is a divine person; yet there are not three ultimate monarchies, but only one, the holy Trinity. For though each of the three is a divine person, each is also essentially related to the other two divine persons such that none alone is God the Trinity."[27]

The problem of equivocation in the use of the word *God*— for each of the three above explanations involves using *God* in two slightly different ways in the two verses of the Athanasian Creed—is "no particular problem: verses 15 and 16 do not form an argument that would be invalidated by equivocation. They rather make a sequence of confessional assertions that, on the reading just offered, need to be understood precisely in order that their coherence might be preserved."[28] Tritheism is also clearly not a problem here, unless one has determined beforehand that the very idea of three fully personal entities is tritheist. Historically, however, tritheism was, as Plantinga points out, the Arian view that there are three divine persons, two of which are ontologically inferior to and created by the first, but all of whom are worshipped as God. Arianism taught the worship of "second-rate divinity" and, thus, was

[27] Ibid., 52.
[28] Ibid., 51–52.

polytheistic. Worship belongs only to God, but in Arianism, the Son and Spirit, who were creatures of the Father and so entirely separate beings both from each other and from the Father, are nevertheless treated as equal to the Father—as gods and objects of worship. Arianism taught the worship of one God and two creatures all in the name of God. That is certainly tritheism and polytheism.

Plantinga closes with the affirmation that the social view is in fact the biblical analogy, for in the Bible the Church as one body but many members is the analogy suggested by Christ in John 17:21.

INTERACTING WITH PLANTINGA'S VIEW

Although Plantinga seems to contradict Van Til's approach to the Trinity, regarding as "impossible to hold" the position of Augustine which Van Til basically follows, close consideration of his view suggests that he may not be as far from Van Til as he first appears.

Contributions of Plantinga's View

What has Plantinga actually offered us here? I think that he offers us at least three things. First, Plantinga has added his voice and the weight of his name to those who regard Barth's doctrine as modalistic. Barth's view, as Plantinga points out, precludes the biblical doctrine of a God who is love, though it is certain that Barth and his followers certainly wish for such a God. Plantinga might have said of Barth, as he said of Augustine, that he is more confused than in error, but, in fact, he comes down harder on Barth because, I suspect, there is much less excuse at this point in the discussion for the kind of misinterpretation exhibited in Barth's doctrine. Maybe, too, he thinks that Barth ought to be aware of the danger of his views, though he asserts them with evident self-consciousness. However that may be, Barth's view is found to be utterly inadequate either to do what Barth himself wishes to accomplish with his doctrine or to represent the teaching of the Bible.[29]

Second, with regard to Augustine, Plantinga provides important material for thought and, perhaps, a legitimate criticism, whether we wish to follow Plantinga all the way or not. In making this criticism, Plantinga is not by any means alone, as can be seen, for example, by the following quotations from Colin Gunton:

> Augustine is at his weakest in his treatment of the persons of the Trinity, flattening out their distinctiveness, partly because he does not appreciate the weight being borne by the Cappadocian concept of hypostasis or person, partly because the concept of relation is simply inadequate as an equivalent—only a person can be personal; and a relation is not a person—and partly because in distinction from Richard of St. Victor he seeks the human analogue of the Trinity not in the loving relation of persons to each other but inside the

---

[29] Pannenberg concludes that Barth's doctrine is not actually derived from the Scriptures themselves, but from Barth's concept of revelation: "In fact, however, the *Church Dogmatics* does not develop the doctrine of the trinitarian God from the data of the historical revelation of God as Father, Son, and Spirit, but from the formal concept of revelation as self-revelation, which, as Barth sees it, entails a subject of revelation, an object, and revelation itself, all of which are one and the same. This model of a Trinity of revelation is easily seen to be structurally identical with that of the self-conscious Absolute, especially when God's revelation has to be viewed primarily as a self-revelation. The subject of the revelation is only one. Barth could thus think of the doctrine of the Trinity as an exposition of the subjectivity of God in his revelation. This being so, there is no room for a plurality of persons in the one God but only for different modes of being in the one divine subjectivity" (Wolfhart Pannenberg, *Systematic Theology*, trans. Geoffrey W. Bromiley [Grand Rapids: Eerdmans, 1991], 1:296). Also, "Barth did not develop the trinitarian statements out of the content of the revelation to which scripture bears witness but out of the formal concept that is expressed in the above statement" (304). Van Til observes further that Barth's revelational concept itself is existential rather than biblical with results that are fundamentally antitrinitarian. Cf. *The New Modernism* (Philadelphia: Presbyterian and Reformed, 1947), 147–48.

head of the one individual, in the structure of the mind's intellectual love of itself.[30]

For all of Origen's attempt to write plurality into the being of things through the concept of the eternal spirits, there is no doubt that for him the plurality that is the mark of the finite world is a defect of being. Plurality is inherently problematic. Further, the world of becoming, materiality and time is created in order to provide a place of punishment and correction for the fallen spirits, in some contrast to Irenaeus' celebration of the goodness of the created order which was created as a blessing. The tendency to a rather gnostic view of matter is to be found in Augustine, too. Despite his averrals of the goodness and reality of the created order, the sensible world is for him manifestly inferior to the intellectual—that Platonic dualism is never long absent from his writing—while the oneness of God is manifestly elevated over the plurality of the Trinity. It is symptomatic of his suspicion of plurality that the material world is rejected as manifestly inferior to the spiritual in providing analogies for the being of God. What we see in the Origenist-Augustinian tradition is an elevation of the one over the many in respect of transcendental status. Unity, but not plurality, is transcendental. The elevation of the one is most clearly visible in the thought of Aquinas, whom I shall use as my main illustration of the downgrading of the many.[31]

Gunton's understanding of the influence of Plato on Augustine is more comprehensive than Plantinga's, or at least more comprehensive than what Plantinga has the space to deal with in a short article. Whether the central problem has to do with the doctrine of simplicity, as Plantinga suggests, or is a broader problem, as Gunton sees it, the fact remains that in the end Augustine is criticized for not being wholly faithful

---

[30] *The Promise of Trinitarian Theology*, 94.
[31] *The One, the Three and the Many*, 137–38.

to the biblical affirmation of the personal plurality of God. If we assume that Gunton and Plantinga are correct on this point, their critique has profound implications for the doctrine of the Trinity itself, for our understanding of its history and impact in the West, and for its application in our day to the Christian worldview.

Third, Plantinga offers us what he believes is a more biblical presentation of the doctrine of the Trinity. On this point, his approach is undoubtedly helpful. The social analogy is found in the Bible; Augustine's psychological analogy is not. Indeed, the social analogy seems to be part of the very essence of what it means that man is created in God's image, for we certainly image the plurality in God not as individuals,[32] but as social groups. The family and the Church are both explicitly related to the fellowship of the persons of the Trinity (Gen. 1:26–27; Jn. 17:21) and should thus be regarded as God-given analogies.

Questions for Plantinga's View

Plantinga's essay also raises numerous questions, some of which are difficult to answer. To begin with, How far may we trust analogies to give us insight into the Trinity? A related question is, Should the family analogy stand alone? In Scripture, it is common to illustrate the same truth from many different perspectives. The Church is the bride of Christ, the body of Christ, the new Temple, the branches of the Vine, the new Israel, the new priesthood, etc. Any one of

---

[32] It is worth noting that William G. T. Shedd believed that Augustine's psychological analogy was correctly understood to imply a plurality of divine persons since man must reflect God both as an individual and as a society. "Augustine contended that man was made in the image of the triune God, the God of revelation; not in that of the God of natural religion, or the untriune deity of the nations. Consequently, it was to be expected that a trinitarian analogue can be found in his mental constitution, which he attempted to point out" (*Dogmatic Theology* [reprint, Minneapolis: Klock & Klock, 1979], 1:261).

these analogies taken alone might be subject to philosophical or practical abuse. Taken together, they mutually qualify one another, supplying the deficiencies of each other, so to speak. By using multiple analogies, some of the problems we encounter when attempting to illustrate the doctrine of the Trinity may be avoided. The Bible itself offers us more than one analogy to the Trinity. To add just one analogy to that of the family, Vern Poythress, following the lead of the linguist Kenneth L. Pike, develops the trinitarian implications of John 1:1. The Father speaks the Word, the Son is the spoken Word, and the Spirit is the Breath that carries the Word.[33]

Second, Plantinga attempts to take away the logical offense provoked by traditional statements of the doctrine of the Trinity. But his own formula, simply stated, comes to this: God possesses one essence and God possesses three essences.[34] Similarly, by suggesting that the two verses of the Athanasian Creed involve equivocation on the meaning of the word *God*, Plantinga offers a formula that can be paraphrased as "three who are called God, but one God." Thus, while Plantinga seems enthusiastically opposed to any statement of the Trinity that requires us to believe what is candidly paradoxical, it is not at all evident that his own formulation succeeds in being genuinely scrutable.

Third, a related problem concerns the definition and number of divine essences. On Plantinga's view, what is a

[33] I am grossly simplifying the analogy. In his syllabus, *The Supremacy of God in Interpretation* (available from the Westminster Campus Bookstore, P.O. box 1073 / 2960 W. Church Road, Glenside, PA 19038), Vern S. Poythress offers an extended and detailed analysis of John 1:1 that goes far beyond what I suggest here.

[34] This is derived from his statement: "Each of Father, Son, and Spirit possesses, then, the whole generic divine essence and a personal essence that distinguishes that person from the other two. Both kinds of essence unify. The generic essence assures that each person is fully divine. The personal essences relate each to the other in unbroken, unbreakable love and loyalty" ("TOPT," 51–52).

divine essence and how many essences does God have? One? Four? Does it really help us to run from a doctrine which might be construed to imply that there are four persons in God to find shelter in a doctrine which might be construed to imply that there are four essences in God? Have we here made great progress?

Fourth, how do we state Plantinga's view in more detail? He prefers not to say that the Father, the Son, and the Spirit are each identical to the divine essence. How then shall we think about all of this? Are the persons each identical to the personal essence they possess? The answer would seem to be affirmative, for it is their personal essences which identify them. How then do they also possess another essence, which is not identical with their person? Which essence is more "essential"?

The point of these questions is just to say that the more I consider the view in detail, the less confident I am that Plantinga has given us a formula which relieves us of logical strain. It may be that what he offers is simply a new and different vocabulary that promises more than it delivers, thus leaving us not only with very much the same mystery we have always had, but also more encumbered with the burden of ferreting out the problems concealed in the new terminology.

Fifth, one more potential problem of Plantinga's explanation of the essences of God is the problem of "composition." Plantinga's view seems to lend itself at least to the notion that God is a *combination* of essences. For how could we be said to have the Trinity if one of the essences is missing? Certainly in the orthodox view, too, the word *Trinity* is not applied to the individual persons, but the notion that each of the three persons is coterminous with the divine being prevents any notion of composition. When there is a multiplicity of essences, the problem takes on a different form since essences seem to be separable "things." In

Plantinga's view, it seems like we are required to have three personal essences and one generic divine essence all "combined" before we have the Trinity.

Sixth, what does Plantinga's doctrine of four essences mean for the doctrine of the attributes of God? Any doctrine of God which claims that attributes belong only to God's essence and not to the several persons would seem to be denying that the Father loves the Son in a manner distinct from the way that the Son loves the Father. And this seems to deny that the relationship of love is truly personal. Does Plantinga view the attributes as belonging in any way at all to the personal essences? It would seem that he would, or at least could. But if he does, it raises another problem—namely, How do the attributes of the personal essences relate to the attributes of the generic essence?

Finally, there is the question of tritheism. We must not only ask whether or not Plantinga has taken sufficient care to avoid the danger of this heresy, we also have to consider exactly what tritheism might be. Plantinga himself suggests that the essential issue in the problem of tritheism is not whether the persons of the Trinity are each identical to the divine essence, so that there is clearly one and only one God—the essential issue according to many if not most theologians[35]—but, rather, the problem of subordinationism. Arians, Plantinga says, were the tritheists, for they believed that the Father, Son, and Spirit were of three utterly different essences, the Son and the Spirit being creatures.

But is Plantinga's definition adequate for our day, and has he taken sufficient care to avoid tritheism? Does his view

---

[35] Shedd offers a common, though perhaps debatable, view of tritheism. "The trinitarian persons are not so real as to constitute three essences, or beings. This is the error of tritheism. If 'real,' which is derived from *res*, be taken in its etymological signification, then the distinction is to be called modal, not real. A trinitarian person is a mode of a thing (*res*), and not a separate thing" (*Dogmatic Theology*, 1:280).

imply that the many are more ultimate than the one, that God is three in a way that is fundamentally more important than the way in which He is one? A view that asserts a multiplicity of essences at least invites tritheism. If he would avoid leading the Church toward outright worship of three gods, it is important that he develop further the doctrine of God's unity.

Thomas R. Thompson suggests that the danger of tritheism is only present when: (1) there is the possibility of multiple conflicting wills, or (2) when there is a qualitative difference between the divine persons, as was asserted by the Arians, the first "Christian polytheists."[36] Clearly, if this definition is considered legitimate, Plantinga is not at all guilty of tritheism. William J. Hill, on the other hand, obviously presupposes a different definition of tritheism when he presents the following critique of the social trinitarianism of William Hasker, whose position seems quite similar to Plantinga's:

> Put very simply, the unity Hasker gives to the divine nature is only generic in kind. While allowing that the nature of God is *common* to all three persons, this dissolves any real *identity* of that nature with the persons, singly or severally. . . . The inexorable logic of this position does lead to understanding the members of the Trinity as "participating in" or "sharing" a single nature, rather than being identified in a real and ontic way with it. If this is so, then how is it possible to avoid the implication of tritheism?[37]

[36] See "Trinitarianism Today: Doctrinal Renaissance, Ethical Relevance, Social Redolence," *Calvin Theological Journal* 32 (no. 1, April 1997): 37–38. Plantinga himself refers to the Arians as the real tritheists, but he does not develop the matter like Thompson does, in spite of its being a point that needs discussion and emphasis.

[37] *The Three Personed God: The Trinity as the Mystery of Salvation* (Washington, D.C.: Catholic University of America Press, 1982), 218.

The concerns of Hill are not limited by any means to Roman Catholic theologians. Three persons who merely share the same nature or essence are not ontologically one. The unity they have seems too similar to the unity that is found in the human race, in which multiple persons are all called "human" because they share the same nature. The property of mutual indwelling, however defined, does not seem to go far enough to provide the oneness which the Church has always confessed of God.

Chapter Two
Van Til's Doctrine of the Trinity[1]

Contrary to Plantinga, Van Til seems to revel in the appearance of contradiction. Rather than attempting to relieve the paradox or point the way for reconciliation, Van Til emphasizes it further by using language that is, at first glance, patently contradictory.

It is sometimes asserted that we can prove to men that we are not asserting anything that they ought to consider irrational, inasmuch as we say that God is one in essence and three in person. We therefore claim that we have not asserted unity and trinity of exactly the same thing.

Yet this is not the whole truth of the matter. We do assert that God, that is, the whole Godhead, is one person. We have noted how each attribute is coextensive with the being of God. We are compelled to maintain this in order to avoid the notion of an uninterpreted being of some sort. In other words, we are bound to maintain the identity of the attributes of God with the being of God in order to avoid the specter of brute fact. In a similar manner we have noted how theologians insist that each of the persons of the Godhead is coterminous with the being of the Godhead. But all this is not to say that the distinctions of the attributes are merely nominal. Nor is it to

[1] I am concerned more with certain controversial features of Van Til's view than with his entire presentation.

say that the distinctions of the persons are merely nominal. We need both the absolute cotermineity of each attribute and each person with the whole being of God, and the genuine significance of the distinctions of the attributes and the persons.[2]

Note that Van Til speaks of the simplicity of God, the doctrine of God's attributes being similar to the distinction of the persons, and that he specifically asserts the view that Plantinga ascribes to traditional theology, "God, that is the whole Godhead, is one person." It seems then that Van Til is guilty of all the "errors" that Plantinga ascribes to the Augustinian view.

But Van Til does not stop there. He asserts the threeness of God with all the clarity of Plantinga. Plantinga may or may not be fair when he characterizes Augustine's view of the Trinity as stating that God is three persons, but "really, there are not three distinct divine persons in God at all, but only one—God the Trinity himself, identical with the divine essence."[3] But Van Til cannot be so characterized. He asserts very clearly that the threeness of God is *equally ultimate* with the oneness of God. Any compromise of the ultimacy of God's threeness would be utterly destructive of Van Til's whole project. It would ruin not only his view of the Trinity, but the application of the Trinity to the Christian worldview which Van Til is attempting to secure.

For what Van Til seeks is nothing less than to establish the doctrine of the Trinity as the foundation for Christian theology and the Christian worldview. To do so, he applies his view of the Trinity to the traditional philosophical problem of the one and the many, claiming that the doctrine of the Trinity is

---

[2] *An Introduction to Systematic Theology* (Philipsburg, N.J.: Presbyterian and Reformed, 1978), 229. Hereafter referred to as *IST*.
[3] "TOPT," 47.

the biblical solution to this philosophical problem.[4] In God, the one and the many are equally ultimate. Neither oneness nor threeness can have any sort of priority. For Van Til, this also means that the doctrine of the Trinity is the ground for a Christian approach to knowledge. Just as no man can fully comprehend the triune God, no man can by mere reason or intuition figure out the solution to the problem of the one and the many. It must be revealed. The ultimate answer to the riddle of reality can only come as a gift from the God who is Himself that answer—the God who created all things to reveal His glory. Only an epistemology grounded in revelation from the triune God offers an ultimate solution to the problem of the one and the many, and therefore a coherent and meaningful worldview.

Though some have received Van Til's view enthusiastically, others have been deeply offended. Van Til has been accused of holding a heretical view of the Trinity, or at least of employing a novel formulation that creates misunderstanding. His paradoxical view is said to undermine rather than provide a foundation for a Christian theory of knowledge. Some have even denied the connection between the doctrine of the Trinity and the problem of the one and the many, which would seem to be applicable no matter what one's view of the Trinity.

---

[4] To state it simply, the world created by God reflects the complexity of God Himself. There is multiplicity of things in the world, but since these things fall into various categories, we must speak of unities as well. Knowledge of the world depends upon there being unity so that we can relate the diverse things and facts that we encounter. At the same time, the diverse facts and things themselves must have real meaning, too, lest they become wholly absorbed into theoretical unities. Unity and diversity must both be real and have ultimate meaning in order for anything to have meaning. Why is the world so? Because it was created by a God who is both one and many—who is equally one and many, ultimately and unchangeably one and many. The world is reflecting Him. How can we find the harmony of the one and the many in our knowledge of the world and in our relationships with it and one another? By living in obedience to the God who created all and gave us His word to show us the way.

The Problem of Contradiction

Does Van Til present a view of the Trinity that is really contradictory? Has he exaggerated the problem and made it more difficult for Christians both to believe and to defend the doctrine of the Trinity? I think not. On the contrary, it seems to me that Van Til takes the problem far more seriously than those who offer facile suggestions for removing the apparent contradiction. For the problem is actually much deeper and more serious than most acknowledge. To illustrate this requires us to turn from Van Til to consider others' attempts to solve the problem.

An exception to general evangelical neglect of the theology of the Trinity is Millard J. Erickson's *God in Three Persons: A Contemporary Interpretation of the Trinity.*[5] Erickson is helpful because he refers to and evaluates most of the major names in recent trinitarian discussion. Oddly, he does not refer to or interact with Plantinga in spite of holding a "social" view of the Trinity and being interested in stating the doctrine in a manner that avoids contradiction. Nor does he refer to or interact with Van Til in spite of his desire to show how the doctrine of the Trinity relates to the Christian life. But Erickson does devote considerable attention to the problem of apparent contradiction, and his discussion is helpful for our consideration of Van Til.

Erickson refers to Stephen Davis, who summarizes the doctrine of the Trinity in five statements and then shows the contradictory implications of these statements.[6] Davis' approach is important because the doctrine of the Trinity is not simply the doctrine that "God is one in one sense and three in another," as some have said. In fact, the word *Trinity* is simply

---

[5] Millard J. Erickson, *God in Three Persons: A Contemporary Interpretation of the Trinity* (Grand Rapids: Baker, 1995). Hereafter referred to as *GTP*.
[6] Ibid., 130–31.

a convenient handle we use to succinctly summarize a number of truths taught in the Bible. And when we list those truths, as Davis does, the apparent inconsistency is clear. We confess that the Bible teaches the following:

(1) The Father is God.
(2) The Son is God.
(3) The Spirit is God.
(4) The Father is not the Son and the Son is not the Holy Spirit and the Holy Spirit is not the Father.
(5) There is one and only one God.

These statements "seem to constitute an inconsistent set, that is, a set of statements not all of whose members can be true." Statements (1), (2), (3), and (5) entail the following:

(6) The Father, the Son, and the Holy Spirit are one thing.

But statement (4) entails:

(7) The Father, the Son, and the Holy Spirit are separate things.

Erickson enumerates the same three alternatives that Plantinga does. Modalism tries to resolve the problem by modifying statement (4) in such a way that it is seen not to entail (7). Barth, Rahner, Jenson, and others offer a solution that at least tends in this direction. The opposite approach, tritheism, escapes the problem of contradiction by modifying statements (1), (2), (3), and (5) in such a way that they no longer entail (6). Plantinga and the social trinitarians offer a solution that may be understood to tend in this direction. Traditional Christianity offers a more complex answer.

Erickson himself takes an approach that is similar to
Plantinga's, though, as I said, he does not mention him.

> The Godhead is to be thought of less as a unity, in the
> sense of oneness of simplicity, than as a union, involving
> three persons, Father, Son, and Holy Spirit. Without each
> of these, God would not be. Each is essential to the life of
> the Father and Spirit, or as Son and Spirit, without the
> third of these persons in that given case. Further, none of
> these could exist without being part of the Trinity. There
> would be no basis of life, apart from this union. Thus, in
> speaking of union, there should be no inference combin-
> ing that which antecedently existed, prior to coming to-
> gether. None has the power of life within itself alone.
> Each can only exist as part of the Triune God.[7]

One of the problems of the social view is apparent here already, for twice in this short quotation Erickson refers to the
persons as "parts" of God, suggesting that the doctrine of divine simplicity can not be so simply dispensed with. Is God
composed of parts? In a view that wishes to emphasize the
persons, must we speak of them as "itself?"

More important for our immediate discussion is Erickson's
attempt to avoid contradiction in his statement of the doctrine of the Trinity. Part of his approach is linguistic. He suggests that the word "is" may have different meanings, the "is"
of identity, the "is" of inclusion, and the "is" of attribution.[8]
Erickson claims,

> When, however, we speak of the individual members of
> the Trinity we are working with a different use of "is."

---

[7] Ibid., 264.

[8] Ironically, Erickson offers as one of the examples of the various senses of
the word "is" the sentence, "Bill Clinton is the president of the United States."
Given the president's attempt to defend himself from criticism by asking what
was meant by "is," Erickson's was a politically relevant discussion of the Trinity.

When we say, for example, "The Father is God," we are not using the "is" of identity. If that were the case, we would be saying, "The Father equals God." It is not invertible to say, "God is (or equals) the Father." For if that were true, then when we say, "The Son is God," and "The Holy Spirit is God," we would be saying, "The Son equals God," and "The Holy Spirit equals God." When we invert then, we would have "God is the Father, "God is the Son," and "God is the Holy Spirit," which would clearly lead us into the type of contradiction that the doctrine of the Trinity is thought to represent.[9]

As a matter of fact, it is the traditional orthodox view of the Trinity, found in both Roman Catholic and Protestant writers, that each of the Three persons is identical with the whole essence of God. Thus Bavinck writes,

This idea was developed by Augustine. He does not derive the trinity from the Father but from the unity of the divine essence: from the "godhead," neither does he conceive of it as accidental but as essential to the being of God. According to him the trinitarian mode of existence pertains to God's very essence. *In that respect personality is identical with God's being itself.* "For to God it is not one thing to be, another to be a person, but it is absolutely the same thing." For if essence pertains to God in an absolute sense, but personality only in a relative sense, then the three persons could not constitute one being. *Hence, every person is identical with the entire being and equal to the other two persons taken together or to all the three. With creatures this is different. One person does not equal three,* "but in God it is not so; for the Father, the Son, and the Holy Spirit together are not a greater essence than the Father alone or the Son alone; but these three substances or persons, if they must be so termed, together are equal to each singly." In the highest trinity one is as

---

[9] *GTP*, 265–66.

much as the three together, nor are two anything more than one;
moreover they are infinite in themselves. So both each is in
each, and all are in each, and each is in all, and all are in all,
and all are one. . . . So also the being of God does not differ essentially or substantially from the first person, the
second person, or the third person. It differs "in reason,
in relationship." One and the same being is and is called
Father when viewed in his relation to that same being in
the person of the Son. And the persons severally differ
only in this respect, that the one is Father, the other Son
and the third Spirit.[10]

Erickson, then, like Plantinga, attempts to escape contradiction by rejecting the Augustinian view of the Trinity, which
has been followed by most Roman Catholic and Protestant
theologians. Which is to say that the problem of stating the
doctrine of the Trinity in clearly noncontradictory terms is a
much larger problem than is often thought. This remains true
even after Plantinga and Erickson offer suggestions to revise
the doctrine. However, whether or not they are correct in
their attempted revision, it is clear that when Van Til urges
that the doctrine is inescapably paradoxical, *he is being impec-*
cably orthodox.

It is also significant that, in the end, Erickson concedes
that even after revising it, he cannot state the doctrine of the
Trinity in terms that are altogether straightforward. Despite
what may be thought to be the advantages of a social view, he
concludes:

It may also be necessary, in order to convey the unusual
meaning involved in this doctrine, to utilize what
analytical philosophers would term "logically odd

---

[10] Herman Bavinck, *The Doctrine of God* (Edinburgh: Banner of Truth Trust,
1977), 302–3. Emphasis added. Much more to the same effect could be quoted
from Bavinck or other Reformed theologians.

language." This means using language in such a way as intentionally to commit grammatical errors. Thus, I have sometimes said of the Trinity, "He are three," or "They is one." For we have here a being whose nature falls outside our usual understanding of person, and that nature can perhaps only be adequately expressed by using language that calls attention to the almost paradoxical character of the concepts.[11]

Returning to Van Til, we may have a better idea of his reasons for embracing rather than fleeing from the apparent contradiction. I do not mean that Van Til believed the doctrine of the Trinity was a *true* contradiction, nor am I implying that he espoused irrationalism. On the contrary, on this point Van Til is entirely in sympathy with Plantinga. If a belief is patently nonsense, no Christian can or should try to believe it, for the God of the Bible is wholly rational. He writes, for example:

An especially dangerous form in which the confusion between divine and human knowledge obtains today is in the recent discussions on the question of mystery. So, for instance, the late Professor Donald Mackenzie of Princeton has written a book *Christianity: The Paradox of God,* in which he confuses the modern concept of the ultimate mysteriousness of the universe with the Christian concept of the incomprehensibility of God. Yet there is no more than a verbal similarity between the two. The church's doctrine of the incomprehensibility of God is based upon and is the logical consequence of God's absolute self-existence. It is just because God is an eternal and self-contained being while we are his temporal creatures that we cannot ever hope to comprehend his being. But this absolute incomprehensibility of God, just because it is based upon God's absolute rationality, is not

[11] *GTP*, 270.

inconsistent with the genuine rational character of our knowledge. On the contrary, our knowledge is rational because God is ultimately rational. At the same time, God is incomprehensible to us because he is ultimately rational. It is not because God is irrational that we cannot comprehend him; it is because God is rational, and in the nature of the case, ultimately rational, that we cannot comprehend him. It is not because God is darkness that he is incomprehensible to us, but it is because he is light, and, in the nature of the case, absolute light. God dwelleth in a light that no man can approach unto. We are not blind because of the light of God; it is only in God's light that we see light.[12]

There is nothing hidden in God, nothing which God does not fully comprehend. Whatever appears to be irrational or paradoxical only appears so to us because we finite creatures can never obtain all the necessary data, do not have the kind of "data cruncher" necessary to comprehend the rationality of all things, and cannot perceive the relations among the almost infinite bits of data—not to mention the fact that sin, too, clouds our reasoning. But in God, all is rational and rationally known. Obviously, this includes the truth of God's own being. Though we cannot comprehend all, our worldview is not irrational because it is grounded in a God who is absolutely rational.

Therefore, what we have in Van Til is a notion similar to that of Stephen Davis. Davis concludes that the doctrine of the Trinity is beyond our comprehension. But he does not take that to mean that it is irrational or contradictory. A contradiction is "an inconsistent statement of the form 'p and not-p,' where there is no suggested or available amplification of the terms in the statement that removes the contradiction

---

[12] *IST*, 12.

[sic] or shows that it is only apparent."[13] Davis regards the Trinity as a "mystery" which he defines as "an apparent contradiction which there is good reason to believe."[14] It is rational to believe a "mystery" if there is good reason to believe the contradiction is not real but only apparent. In the case of the doctrine of the Trinity, the biblical teaching about God's perfect knowledge of Himself and all things implies His perfect rationality. Furthermore, the doctrine of God's transcendence and incomprehensibility includes the notion that we cannot fully comprehend Him, even though our limited knowledge of Him is true. Thus, we have good reason to believe that the doctrine of the Trinity is not actually but only apparently contradictory.

Davis adds that we should only believe in a mystery if there are strong reasons for believing it, apart from the question of its coherence. Again, all the reasons that lead us to believe in the truth of the Christian religion induce us also to believe that the doctrine of the Trinity is true. Van Til would add that, apart from faith in the triune God of Scripture, it is impossible to possess true knowledge of anything at all. Finally, to reiterate, Van Til's statement of the doctrine does not imply that God is irrational, for Van Til's view assumes that there is a hidden and humanly undefinable "amplification" of the terms or the statements that resolves the contradiction. Unless we are going to condemn Augustine's doctrine as heretical, too, we will have to say that Van Til is absolved from the charge of "unitarian heresy." However, he may still be guilty of "novelty."[15]

---

[13] Qtd. in *GTP*, 256.

[14] Qtd. in *GTP*, 257. The whole discussion of Davis is taken from Erickson.

[15] John W. Robbins, *Cornelius Van Til: The Man and the Myth* (Jefferson, Md.: The Trinity Foundation, 1986), 20–21.

The Question of Novelty

I think that it is clear from the larger context of Van Til's writings that he employs his unusual formula for a purpose. But before we turn to that, it is also relevant to observe that he had precedent. First, Plantinga makes the point for us when he summarizes the traditional view from Augustine to the present:

> As the examples from Book 15 show, Augustine does hold that there are three persons in God. But he also holds, even if he doesn't say so, that there is only one such person. For if the Father, Son, and Spirit are all identical with the divine essence, if they are not just instances of it or particularized exemplifications of it, then it follows that none is a person distinct from the other.[16]

Van Til, judged by Plantinga's analysis, has correctly summarized the teaching of Augustine. Plantinga even says, "People who take this middle position *often* construe the orthodox claim as holding that in God each of Father, Son, and Spirit is a distinct person; yet they aren't three persons but one."[17] Add to this the similarity between the paragraph from Plantinga above, our previous quotation of Bavinck (pp. 47–48 above), and the following quotation from Bavinck, "the three persons are *one divine personality* brought to complete self-unfoldment, a self-unfoldment which arises out of and takes place by means of and within the divine essence."[18] Clearly, Van Til's formula is no less accurate as a summary of Bavinck.

---

[16] "TOPT," 46. Thomas R. Thompson says, "God, therefore, in most Catholic treatments is, on the one hand, a Trinity of persons in some ontological and/or relational sense, but finally one person in terms of consciousness, even if any trinitarian members maintain a 'relative identity'" ("Trinitarianism Today," 29, note 79).

[17] "TOPT," 43.

[18] *The Doctrine of God*, 301.

The Augustinian view which Bavinck and Van Til hold may be wrong, as Plantinga urges, but it is rather late to label it as "novel."

Although Van Til no doubt has both Bavinck and Augustine in mind—as may be seen in the paragraph in which he introduces the expression "God, that is, the whole Godhead, is one person"—a careful perusal of his sources suggests that he almost certainly adopted the "one person" formula to express the doctrine of one of his favorite Princeton theologians, whose work he quotes a few pages before, that "radical innovator" Charles H. Hodge:

> The third point decided concerning the relation of the persons of the Trinity, one to the other, relates to their union. As the essence of the Godhead is common to the several persons, they have a common intelligence, will, and power. There are not in God three intelligences, three wills, three efficiencies. The three are one God, and therefore have one mind and will. This intimate union was expressed in the Greek church by the word περιχώρησις, which the Latin words *inexistentia, inhabitatio,* and *intercommunio,* were used to explain. These terms were intended to express the Scriptural facts that the Son is in the Father, and the Father in the Son; that where the Father is, there Son and Spirit are; that what the one does the others do. . . . So also what the one knows, the others know. . . . A common knowledge implies *a common consciousness.*
>
> This fact—of the intimate union, communion, and inhabitation of the persons of the Trinity—is the reason why everywhere in Scripture, and instinctively by all Christians, God as God is addressed as a person, in perfect consistency with the Tripersonality of the Godhead. We can and do pray to each of the Persons separately; and we pray to God as God; for the three persons are one

God, one not only in substance, but in knowledge, will, and power. [19]

The first paragraph above is quoted in Van Til's discussion. The content of the second paragraph is reproduced in Van Til's description of God as "one person." Van Til has stated the matter more boldly than Hodge, but he is clearly drawing out the implications of the Augustinian doctrine, especially as he finds it in Bavinck, and reproducing the theology of Hodge in modified language. "Novel," then, is not the right word for Van Til's view. What he has done is express the traditional view with only slightly nontraditional expressions. Those who understand the substance of the matter and are not obsessed with the words should not have problems with Van Til[20]—unless, like Plantinga, they object to Augustine, Bavinck, and many of the greatest theologians in the history of the Church.

The Purpose of Paradox

I believe that Van Til has reasons for the language he uses. I believe we can distinguish three classes of reasons, but I have less evidence for the first, which is the pedagogical. The pedagogical class appears to include two reasons. First, Van Til frequently drew attention to the fact that we must express Christian theology in the language of our day. Since his own expression of the doctrine of the Trinity sets his view in as radical a contrast as is possible with Barthian and other nonpersonal or anti-personal views of God, it may be seen as an attempt to communicate unambiguously the totally personal

---

[19] Charles H. Hodge, *Systematic Theology*, 1:461–62. Emphasis added. Qtd. in *IST* on page 225.

[20] Calvin writes, "I am quite aware that Christians are lords both of words and of all things, and can therefore apply words to things as they choose, provided a pious sense be kept, even though there may be some incorrect usage in speaking" (*Institutes*, 4:19:1).

character of God. "God is not," as Van Til emphasizes, "an essence that has a personality; He is absolute personality. Yet, within the being of the one person we are permitted and compelled by Scripture to make the distinction between a specific or generic type of being, and three personal subsistences."[21] Second, perhaps Van Til intends to force his students and readers to think by using language that they were unaccustomed to.

The second class of reasons is theological and philosophical. As we have already explained, Van Til sees the doctrine of the Trinity as the ultimate answer to the problem of the one and the many. God must be one no less than He is three and three no less than He is one. Neither His threeness nor His oneness can take priority in time or logic over the other. According to Van Til, the oneness and threeness of God must be "equally ultimate." If Plantinga is correct that Augustine in the end gives priority to the one over the many, on this point Van Til's disagreement with Augustine would be fundamental. For to give priority to either would be to undermine the entire Christian worldview.

Colin E. Gunton, who seems not to be acquainted with Van Til at all, also treats the doctrine of the Trinity as the solution to the problem of the one and the many. It seems so natural to relate the philosophical problem of the one and the many with the biblical doctrine of the Trinity that one would think theologians through the centuries would have addressed the subject frequently and in detail. Such is not the case. Though often discussed by philosophers,[22] theologians have not given it the attention it deserves. Gunton's 1992 Bampton Lectures,

---

[21] *IST*, 229–30. Note that this explanation is contrary to the typical Augustinian approach, which avoids the notion of a "generic type of being."

[22] Lois De Raeymaiker, for example, writes: "Since philosophy seeks above all for a solution to the problem of the one and the many, which is presented moreover under various forms, it ought to determine accurately the nature of

however, are an exception. Gunton treats the problem of the
one and the many as a fundamental cultural problem, and the
Augustinian solution, understood as favoring the one over the
many, as one source for the problems of the modern worldview. His explanation of the problem includes language that
echoes Van Til. And to contrast the one and the many, he
makes use of the views of the same two ancient philosophers
Van Til often refers to.

> The question of the one and the many takes us to the very
> beginnings of philosophy and theology. The contribution
> it makes to the argument is most clearly set forth in the
> famous   disagreement   between   Heraclitus   and
> Parmenides. Our information about the teaching of these
> two founts of Western philosophy is fragmentary and
> often obscure, but it is as representative figures that they
> are of interest to us. Associated with the former is the
> view that everything is flux, and that war is the universal
> creative and ruling force, reality being suffused by forces
> pulling in both ways at once, so that the basic fact in the
> natural world is strife. Although there is for this
> philosopher a world order and not a radical pluralism,
> Guthrie points out that for Heraclitus the fire that
> animates all things, the logos of the universe, is not a
> permanent substratum that remains the same in all its
> modifications, as it was for Aristotle. That would
> introduce rest and stability. On the contrary, Heraclitus
> is the philosopher of plurality and motion: the many are
> prior to the one, and in such a way that there is to be
> found in nature no stability. Parmenides represents the

the unities which it studies." *The Philosophy of Being* (St. Louis: B. Herder,
1954), 62. Gordon Clark saw the problem of the one and the many as the very
beginning of philosophy: "Philosophy begins with the reduction of multiplicity
to unity" (*Thales to Dewey: A History of Philosophy* [1957; reprint, Grand Rapids:
Baker, 1980], 6). For a discussion of this theme in modern thought, see
Franklin L. Baumer, *Modern European Thought: Continuity and Change in Ideas,
1600–1950* (New York: Macmillan, 1977).

opposite pole of thought. For him the real is the totally unchanging, for so reason teaches, contradicting the appearances presented to the senses. Reality is timelessly and uniformly what it is, so that Parmenides is the philosopher of the One *par excellence*. The many do not really exist, except it be as functions of the One.[23]

Van Til, like Gunton, understands the history of Western philosophy and our modern dilemma in terms of the problem of the one and the many. Also like Gunton, Van Til believes that the doctrine of the Trinity offers the only solution. Unlike Gunton, however, Van Til seems to believe that any statement of the doctrine of the Trinity that adequately expresses it as an ultimate solution to the problem of the one and the many must appear contradictory to man since God Himself is incomprehensible. Thus, Van Til develops the doctrine of the Trinity in language that forces man to humble himself before divine revelation. We may confess what is beyond our comprehension and worship God in language that transcends our understanding. What is most important is that we be faithful to God's self-revelation in Scripture.

This brings us to the third class of reasons, which we might call the "evangelical" ones. The apparently contradictory language Van Til employs merely challenges us up front and from the beginning with the kind of problems that Erickson sees hidden under the rocks. Van Til's approach demands of his readers no sacrifice of intellect. What it does demand is a surrender of the pretense of intellectual autonomy from the start, not at the end of a process that first promises to respect man's intellectual autonomy but finally ends by requiring him to set it aside. According to Van Til, from the very first step we must walk by faith. The only way man can know a God

---

[23] Colin Gunton, *The One, the Three and the Many* (Cambridge: Cambridge University Press, 1993) 17–18.

infinitely beyond his ability to grasp is through revelation. God must come to us and make Himself known. But when He does reveal Himself to us, that revelation is authoritative. It demands that we submit our hearts and minds so that we may be free from sin and see the world as it really is. Since the offense of the Gospel includes the offense of the Trinity, we might as well declare it boldly in thought-provoking terms and make it clear from the beginning that the Gospel we preach must be believed in order to be understood.

Related to this is the fact that Van Til is apparently drawing his formulation from Hodge's statement about prayer. For we do pray unto God as God, without making a conscious distinction between the persons. And such prayer is certainly legitimate. A doctrine of the Trinity that comports with the prayers that we find in Scripture and that we ourselves offer to God is grounded in worship, and is therefore likely to encourage our worship as well. Van Til expressly had in mind a theology that demands that we humble our proud hearts before God—a theology that must be practiced in prayer. We should not be surprised to find an allusion to Hodge and his point about praying to the triune God as to one person in the following polemic context:

> In all this Hordern and DeWolf are true to their method. The method of the one does not differ basically from the method of the other, because both are committed to man as autonomous. Both use the laws of logic in order by them to exclude the claims of the God and the Christ of Scripture. Both have long since made "peace with the law of contradiction." The fourth book of Aristotle's *Metaphysics* is for them more authoritative than is the Bible. For this reason they have argued that God cannot exist in trinitarian fashion. *The law of contradiction would be violated if we held that God consists of three persons to whom one can pray as to one God.* Accordingly, the three persons of

the Trinity as Luther and Calvin believed in them, are reduced to three modes of revelation of the one God by
both Hordern and DeWolf. Both agree with Barth on this
point.[24]

CONCLUSION

Van Til states the traditional doctrine of the Trinity in language that differs from traditional statements. However,
when carefully considered, his view is less "novel" than it may
appear to readers unfamiliar with Van Til's sources. What he
does do that is significantly different is relate the doctrine of
the Trinity to the problem of the one and the many and seek
to make it the center of the Christian worldview. Comparison
of Van Til and Plantinga should further our understanding of
the place of the Trinity in the Christian worldview.

[24] *The Case for Calvinism* (Philadelphia: Presbyterian and Reformed, 1963),
82–83. Emphasis added.

Chapter Three
Comparing Van Til with Plantinga

Comparing Van Til's approach to Plantinga's reveals more agreement than one might first expect. Perhaps the most significant area of agreement is in the understanding of the idea of a person. Here Van Til and Plantinga stand together against Barth, Rahner, and other modern theologians who deny individual, self-conscious awareness to the three persons of the Trinity. For Barth, God is one subject. For both Van Til and Plantinga, God is also three subjects. Second, on the meaning and importance of the notion of perichoresis, the two seem to take essentially the same position. Third, on the question of the one and the many, Plantinga's view is probably in accord with Van Til, or at least can be so understood. They do, however, differ. First, where their views vary most widely is in the matter of logic and the use of logic in understanding the Trinity. This may in fact mean that their similarity in other matters includes subtle but important differences as well. Second, the worldview implications of Van Til's approach are certainly more clear.

PERSON

In Van Til's statement that "God is a one-conscious being, and yet he is also a tri-conscious being,"[1] we see that he rejects

---

[1] *IST*, 220.

Barth and others who claim that the modern notion of "individual self-consciousness" is not involved in the trinitarian conception of a person. However, two points must be noted. First, we are speaking of Van Til's understanding of the biblical teaching, not of whether or not the concept of "person," historically conceived, included the notion of self-consciousness.[2] Second, we are not suggesting that Van Til condones modern notions of the individual. The consensus of scholarship is that the theologians of the ancient Church did not think of "individual self-consciousness" in their idea of a person. But the point here is subtle. The emphasis falls on the word "individual," by which is meant one who is conscious of self without reference to others or independent of his consciousness of others, a distinctly modern and Cartesian notion of the self. As we shall see below, Van Til's assertion that God is "tri-personal" does not carry this modern baggage.

On this point Plantinga, too, is emphatic. He would rather be regarded as tritheistic than deny the full personality of the Father, the Son, and the Spirit, for in the Scriptures there is no question of the fact that the three persons of the Trinity are presented as having fully personal relationships. He writes, "Of course if you think tritheism is the view that there are *three fully divine and fully personal entities in the divine life,* what follows is that all three readings are tritheist. But then so is the Gospel of John. And that's good company in which to be tritheist."[3]

---

[2] For example, Barth writes, "What is called 'personality' in the conceptual vocabulary of the nineteenth century is distinguished from the patristic and mediaeval persona by the addition of the attribute of self-consciousness. This really complicates the whole issue" (*Church Dogmatics* [Edinburgh: T & T Clark, 1975], 1:357).

[3] "TOPT", 53 (emphasis added). The "three readings" referred to are explained above in the section on Plantinga, where he discusses the three possible interpretations of the Athanasian Creed on his view of the Trinity.

Both Van Til and Plantinga understand the persons of the Trinity as being self-aware. The persons of the Trinity love one another and seek the glory and blessing of one another. Since the three persons have a relationship of love with one another, they must also have knowledge of one another as "other," which includes the knowledge of self in distinction from the other. Both men would also emphatically affirm that the persons of the Trinity never exist as "individuals," isolated from the others. They do not enter into a relationship that does not previously exist, nor are they conscious of themselves apart from the web of relationships which constitute the three as one God. That is to say, the biblical doctrine that the Godhead consists of three divine persons cannot be fully appreciated apart from the notion of perichoresis.

PERICHORESIS

Colin Gunton and many modern trinitarians stress the importance of perichoresis—the doctrine that the persons of the Trinity indwell one another.[4] On this point Van Til and Plantinga agree with one another and with Gunton, though for Reformed theology an emphasis on perichoresis is not at all new. For example, Francis Turretin (1623–87), the great Reformed theologian of the seventeenth century, used the word "emperichoresis" and expounded it as an important aspect of the doctrine of the Trinity.[5] Hodge, too, includes a

---

[4] Colin Gunton, *The Promise of Trinitarian Theology*, 131, 137ff, 144ff, 155ff. *The One, the Three and the Many*, 152–53, 163–79, 185–86, etc. It is interesting to note that Gunton refers often to Samuel Taylor Coleridge's writings on the Trinity, found in his complete works, the American edition of which was edited by W. G. T. Shedd. It should also be pointed out that Gunton's interpretation of perichoresis may differ in details from Van Til's or Plantinga's.

[5] Francis Turretin, *Institutes of Elenctic Theology* (Philipsburg, N.J.: Presbyterian and Reformed, 1992), 1:257. Calvin, on the other hand, does not expound the notion of perichoresis, though he has an extended discussion of the Trinity in the *Institutes*. A recently published Reformed theology, Robert L.

discussion of perichoresis (Latin: *inexistentia, inhabitatio,* and *intercommunio*).

For Van Til, the doctrine that each person of the Trinity indwells the others means that the persons of the Trinity are "mutually exhaustive of one another." In other words, the three are united in such a way that each one is "co-terminous" with the whole being of God and with each of the other persons. Therefore, there can be nothing "hidden" in the essence in God. Hodge, whom Van Til quotes, emphasizes the unity resulting from the perichoretic indwelling of the persons so far as to say that the three "have one mind and will" and "a common consciousness."[6] In Van Til's terminology, this is to say that because of the mutual and perfect indwelling of the three in one another, they constitute, in a certain sense, "one person."

For Plantinga, too, the importance of the doctrine of perichoresis is found in the way it brings to expression the unity of God. "Each member is a distinct person, but scarcely an *individual* or *separate* person. For in the divine life there is no isolation, no insulation, no secretiveness, no fear of being transparent to another. Hence there may be penetrating, inside knowledge of the other *as other,* but as co-other, loved other, fellow. Father, Son, and Spirit are 'members one of another' to a superlative degree. . . . There is in the divine life a mysterious, primordial in-ness or oneness relation that is short of a oneness of person but much closer than mere common membership in a class."[7] The unity of God is not, therefore, an abstract unity, nor is it found in some underlying impersonal "substratum" of being. Father, Son, and Spirit indwell one another so perfectly that they know one another

---

Reymond's *A New Systematic Theology of the Christian Faith* (Nashville: Thomas Nelson, 1998), denies that the doctrine of perichoresis is biblical (p. 324).

[6] Ibid.

[7] "TOPT," 50–51. This is a good example of Plantinga's doctrine of the Trinity trespassing the boundaries of normal language and logic.

from the inside. In that sense, the three persons may be said to have "one mind." Plantinga even comes close to saying that the perichoretic indwelling of the three persons makes them, in a way, one person. Perhaps we may contrast the two views by saying that what for Plantinga is *"short* of a oneness of person" is for Van Til *"sort* of a oneness of person." If that is the case, the difference between them on this point may be more a matter of language than substance.

ONE AND MANY

One would think that for either Plantinga or Van Til, the doctrine of the Trinity is relevant to the problem of the one and the many. Perichoresis requires both the ultimacy of the many—for there must be three to indwell one another before there can be a doctrine of perichoresis—and the ultimacy of the one—for in addition to the fact that mutual indwelling means oneness, perichoresis also insists that the three do not exist first as separate substances which come into relation at some later time, but they exist in mutual relationship from the beginning. Without the threeness there could be no unity and without the mutually indwelling unity of the persons, there could be no individual persons, for each of the three persons is what He is in relation to the other two.

Though Plantinga and Van Til understand it somewhat differently, the common possession of the one divine nature by the three persons of the Trinity is seen as another source of divine unity. The fact that the one divine nature belongs to each of the three persons fully and equally means that the doctrine of God's being also relates both to ultimate plurality and unity. Plantinga writes,

[T]he holy Trinity is a transcendent society or community of three fully personal and fully divine entities: the Father, the

Son, and the Holy Spirit or Paraclete. These three are wonderfully unified by their common divinity, by the possession by each of the whole divine essence—including, for instance, the properties of everlastingness and sublimely great knowledge, love and glory. They are also united by their common historical redemptive purpose, revelation, and work. Their knowledge and love are directed not only to their creatures, but also primordially and archetypally to each other. The Trinity is thus a zestful, wondrous community of divine light, love, joy, mutuality, and verve.[8]

Plantinga does not allude to the fact that the problem of the one and the many is central to Western thought and lies at the root of every great philosophical debate. It would be hard to say from the present article whether or not he regards the Trinity as relevant to the subject. For even though the fact that God is both one and many seems obviously applicable to the philosophical issue, Norman Geisler and Paul Feinberg, for example, explicitly deny that the doctrine of the Trinity is relevant.[9]

However, Plantinga's doctrine does fit with Van Til's view of the equal ultimacy of the one and the many in God as the ultimate solution to the problem of the one and the many—better, in fact, than Augustine's view fits, if we assume that recent critiques of Augustine's doctrine are correct.

---

[8] Ibid., 50.

[9] *Introduction to Philosophy: A Christian Perspective* (1980; reprint, Grand Rapids: Baker, 1997), 175–76. In order to demonstrate that the doctrine of the Trinity does not really relate to the problem of the one and the many, they construe the problem in terms that are, it seems to me, odd. In other words, they have defined the problem of the one and the many so that God is ruled out from the beginning. This is what is technically referred to as "not inviting God to the party." This may turn out to be as precarious a method for theology as it was in the ancient world for politics. As Belshazzar discovered, God comes to the party whenever He pleases.

LOGIC

On the question of the logic of the Trinity, Van Til and Plantinga may be said to differ considerably. Augustine's view of the Trinity, which Van Til regards as a profound and biblical statement of the truth of the incomprehensible God, Plantinga dismisses as "self-contradictory" and "necessarily false."[10] Much of the difference on this point might be relieved by a fuller study of the historical question, for Van Til would not have sanctioned a doctrine that is "heavily monist" or "Neo-Platonic."[11] If Augustine's doctrine can be demonstrated to have indeed been "unitarian" in its tendency, then we may assume that Van Til would join Plantinga in rejecting it, for a doctrine of the Trinity that regards the one as more ultimate than the many is fundamentally erroneous. Nevertheless, it is hard to imagine Plantinga tolerating Van Til's paradoxical formulation—however similar his own notion of three personal essences and one essence might seem to be, for the disagreement between Van Til and Plantinga on the problem of logic in the doctrine of the Trinity runs deep. Whereas Plantinga wishes to formulate the doctrine of the Trinity so as to avoid the appearance of contradiction as much as it is possible to do so, Van Til formulates the doctrine in terms that seem to exaggerate the problems, after which he challenges the logic of those who assert a contradiction. The two approaches could not differ more in their basic direction.

Why does Van Til take such an approach? When Van Til demands a fundamental reformation of logic itself, he is simply extending the traditional Christian approach to the Trinity one step further. For what is characteristic of trinitarianism from the beginning is the desire to include in the doctrine of God all that the Bible teaches about God,

[10] "TOPT," 47.
[11] Ibid., 46.

rather than, like the Arians or the modalists, reducing the teaching of the Bible to fit human reason.[12] The Trinity has always been confessed as a mystery that transcends understanding but is believed because it is revealed by the transcendent God Himself. Although it is an oversimplification of the theological argument and historical facts, it is not really a distortion of the truth to affirm that it was the heretics who zealously insisted on logic.[13]

Van Til disallows taking Aristotle's notion of contradiction for granted or using it as a standard with which to judge the doctrine of the Trinity. As one of Van Til's followers, Vern Poythress, insists, the biblical doctrine of God both grounds and judges human logic. The doctrine of the Trinity points the way to an epistemology that modifies traditional philosophical logic significantly. We must conclude, then, that from a Van Tillian perspective, to the degree that Plantinga assumes the validity of Aristotle's logic in his attempt to restate the doctrine of the Trinity,[14] his method is worse than futile.

---

[12] See the extended quotation from Hilary in Appendix A. The point appears clearly in the following words from Augustine, " . . . the eye of the human mind, being weak, is dazzled in that so transcendent light, unless it be invigorated by the nourishment of the righteousness of faith. First, however, we must demonstrate, according to the authority of the Holy Scriptures, whether the faith be so" (*On the Trinity*, Book 1, chapter 2). Human reason cannot comprehend the divine mystery apart from faith. The first and most important question, however, is "What does the Scripture teach?"

[13] Thompson writes, "Consistency and coherence, it seems, have proven an elusive commodity in the difficult waters of trinitarian formulation. Indeed, in the history of this doctrine, such logical virtues appear more in the possession of the heretics (e.g., Sabellius and Arius)" ("Trinitarianism Today," 31). It is not my purpose here to imply that Plantinga or other Christians who wish to state the doctrine logically are heretics. Those trinitarians most zealous to state the doctrine logically do not, like Arians and modalists, trim the doctrine down so that it can be neatly circumscribed within the confines of human imagination. It is my purpose to say that the demand to be logical, when pressed too far, leads to a denial not only of the Trinity but of any notion that is beyond man's ken.

[14] It is possible that Plantinga would object to the idea that he is employing Aristotle's logic in his reformulation of the Trinity. However, there is nothing

Strictly speaking in Van Tillian terms, a doctrine of the Trinity grounded in Aristotelian logic constitutes an attack on the whole Christian notion of logic and precludes a truly biblical approach for the formulation of *any* doctrine.

The problem with Aristotle's logic may be illustrated by Poythress' critique of the syllogism or, to state it more properly, his argument on the limitations of man's reason in the use of syllogistic logic.

> The proper operation of syllogisms thus requires the use of univocal terms. A univocal term must cover a perfectly fixed kind of thing, belonging to one or another of Aristotle's basic categories (see Aristotle, *The Categories*). These categories are the fundamental categories of ontology, the beginnings of Aristotle's metaphysics. For the operation of the syllogism Aristotle needs categories that are perfectly fixed and whose boundaries of definition are perfectly sharp. If perfection fails, equivocation enters.
>
> Now such perfection and such absoluteness of knowledge belong only to God. Aristotle tacitly tries to take a divine viewpoint when he uses categories. Each category is an idealization of the actual character of human language. The idealization pushes for a pure classificational aspect, with no need for instantiational and associational aspects. Like the abstract reasoning of Euclid, it aspires to dispense with the knowledge of particular cases (instantiational) and the interaction of persons with knowledge (associational). Moreover, it attempts to arrive at a language of pure information, without an expressive or productive aspect. The syllogistic premises and the syllogistic structures must exist as formulas independent of the personal involvement and influence of

---

in his view that suggests he would make such an objection, and he has not called for anything like a reformulation of logic to fit the Trinity, which is the Van Tillian approach to the problem.

persons who are practitioners of logic—thus the expressive aspect is excised. The syllogistic structure must also exist independent of any concrete application, for the sake of its absolute universality and necessary truthfulness. Only in this way can the reasoning be purely abstract. Hence, Aristotle's categories presuppose the unitarian ontology that we have already analyzed. The categories must collapse instantiation and association into pure classification. They must also collapse expressive and productive aspects into pure information.[15]

If Plantinga takes Aristotle's logic as normative for our understanding of the Trinity—and I say "if" because I am not at all certain that he intends to follow Aristotle—he will have to distort the doctrine at some point, for the knowledge of God cannot be reduced to fit nicely into the categories of human understanding. Van Til requires a reformation of our whole approach to logic, taking the Bible and its doctrine of the Trinity as our norm. This has enormous consequences in the formation of the Christian worldview.

WORLDVIEW

Plantinga indicates from the beginning of his essay that no other doctrine resonates so richly as the doctrine of the Trinity. But he has not really spelled out what the implications of his "social" view of the Trinity might be. For example, one could argue for something more like a socialist view of economics and politics on the basis of the social view of the Trinity, denying the validity of the notion of individual rights. In

---

[15] "Reforming Ontology and Logic in the Light of the Trinity," *Westminster Theological Journal* 57 (no. 1, Spring 1995): 203–4. Poythress aims at a trinitarian method. His categories, instantiation (the Father), classification (the Son), and association (the Spirit) are related to, but not identical with, the expressive (the Father), informational (the Son), and productive (the Spirit) aspects of communication.

other words, Plantinga's doctrine of the Trinity by itself argues for some sort of harmony of the one and the many, but it does not clearly lead us in a particular direction.[16]

Van Til's approach to the Trinity, however, is quite different in that it includes the reformation of logic, demanding that all human thought be subject to the authority of Scripture in order to be truly rational. The fact of man's sinfulness and its impact on reason combine with the inescapable limitations of creaturehood to render it altogether impossible for man to begin with the bare "facts" of nature or history and arrive at truth. Even sinless Adam in the Garden needed revelation from God to know himself and the world around him. In order for man, a creature whose reasoning cannot fathom the complex meaning or design of God's world, to think properly—even apart from the question of sin—he needs divine revelation. This implies that the question of knowledge can never be separated from questions of ethics, for knowledge comes from an Authority to which we owe the most profound submission. Thus, in the Van Tillian perspective, the ethical teaching of the Bible, from Genesis to Revelation, must be brought to bear on every subject.

On this view, attaining the harmony of the one and the many in our knowledge can never be an abstract philosophical project. Worship and obedience, prayer to God and loving our neighbor, in short, all the ethical requirements of Holy

[16] Cf., for example, works such as A. Okechukwu Ogbonnaya, *On Communitarian Divinity: An African Interpretation of the Trinity*; John Schanz, *A Theology of Christian Community*; Juan Luis Segundo, *A Theology for the Artisan of a New Humanity*; Joseph Bracken, *Society and Spirit: A Trinitarian Cosmology* (Selinsgrove, Penn.: Susquehanna UP, 1991); etc. Bracken relates this to physics. "With Harshorne and Cobb, I would argue that atoms and molecules are structured societies of actual occasions, not Aristotelian substances. Yet, with Leclerc I would contend that atoms and molecules do exercise agency. Their agency, however, is in each case not the agency of an individual existent, but rather the collective agency proper to a society, that is, the collation or fusion of all the individual agencies of constituent actual occasions" (*Society and Spirit*, 43).

Scripture are related to even the most abstruse questions of knowledge. This is most obvious in two respects: in the ethical status of the knower, which so largely determines the direction of his thought, and in the nature of understanding as a blessing from God for those who fear Him. But there are other connections that we can neither define or imagine.

Van Til directly challenges the hubris of man's pretended autonomy, which recoils at the very mention of submitting the intellect unto God. He also introduces a view of the Scripture which shows its application to daily life and elevates all life and thought to that which is of the essence of true religion, the offering of ourselves unto God in humble praise.

Insofar as the ramifications of Van Til's doctrine of the Trinity include viewing holy Scripture as a God-given standard for all knowledge, his understanding of the Trinity is more vibrant, rich, and harmonious. For our daily lives, the concrete meaning of faith in a triune God is not a matter of guesswork or obscure speculations. It has been outlined for us in the Bible, which gives us a basic framework within which we are free to move. Just how down-to-earth the doctrine of the Trinity may be is illustrated in another essay[17] by Vern Poythress that sets forth a distinctly trinitarian approach to mathematics.

However, there is one respect in which Van Til's doctrine lacks the concreteness it must have, an important aspect of the doctrine of the Trinity which is, I believe, implicit in Van Til's approach, but which needs to be made explicit to clarify the link between the doctrines of God, creation, revelation, man, and salvation.

---

[17] Vern Poythress, "Mathematics," in *Foundations of Christian Scholarship: Essays in the Van Til Perspective*, ed. Gary North (Vallecito, Calif.: Ross House Books, 1976). Every essay in this very interesting volume applies Van Til's insights into the doctrine of the Trinity to a different academic discipline.

Chapter Four
Kuyper, Covenant, and Worldview

The missing link in Van Til's approach is the Reformed doctrine that the persons of the Trinity are eternally united in a covenantal bond of love. James Jordan supplies the overlooked ingredient when he explains the covenant as "a personal-structural bond which joins the three persons of God in a community of life, and in which man was created to participate."[1] A covenantal relationship among the persons of the Trinity introduces the possibility of a worldview in which the doctrine of God is the fountain from which all other truths flow. The ideal society that Plantinga refers to is the *covenantal* society of the Trinity. Basic worldview themes such as personhood, language, love, freedom, and law are integrated and unified in the personal covenant bond of Father, Son, and Spirit. They are also joined by the covenant bond to the central theme of biblical theology and the organizing structure of systematic theology.

The Trinitarian Covenant in Reformed Theology

Not all Reformed theologians agree that there is such a covenant between the persons of the Trinity. Many who do believe in some sort of trinitarian covenant, commonly called

---

[1] James B. Jordan, *The Law of the Covenant* (Tyler, Tex.: Institute for Christian Economics, 1984), 5. Emphasis in original. Jordan was the first Reformed

"the covenant of redemption," see it as a strictly soteriological covenant. In contrast, Abraham Kuyper regards the
covenant between the persons as an important doctrine for
our understanding of the Trinity—in a manner that is particularly relevant to the concerns of Plantinga's view.

> This danger [tritheism] can be escaped only when the di-
> vine economy of the Three Persons is presented *natura*
> *sua* as a covenant relation. . . . We then confess that in
> the one personality of the divine Essence there consists a
> three-personal distinction, which has in the covenant re-
> lation its unity and an inseparable tie. God Himself is,
> according to this conception, not only of every cov-
> enant, but of the covenant idea as such the living and
> eternal foundation; and the essential unity [of the
> Godhead] has in the covenant relation its conscious ex-
> pression.[2]

Kuyper points the way to an understanding of God that
(1) gives due emphasis to the real distinctions between the
persons of the Trinity, since they must be truly three in order
to be in covenant; (2) brings to light one important aspect of
the personal relationships of the Father, Son and Spirit, for a
covenant is a personal relation of love; (3) clearly places the
doctrine of God at the center of all of Christian theology and
the Christian worldview by linking the doctrine of the Trinity
to all of life by the bond of the covenant, for in Kuyper's

---

writer I read who spoke of the covenant as a Trinitarian relationship. Together
with Poythress and others in the Van Til tradition, Jordan attempts to relate all
of biblical and systematic theology to the doctrine of the Trinity.

   [2] Qtd. in Herman Hoeksema, *Reformed Dogmatics* (Grand Rapids: Reformed
Free Publishing Association), 295. Although Hoeksema disagrees with certain
aspects of Kuyper's formulation, he agrees that the *pactum salutis* gives us insight into the doctrine of the Trinity and he includes his discussion of the *pactum salutis* not under soteriology, but in Christology. He did not, however,
follow through on this insight and develop a wholly covenantal and trinitarian
theology.

view God Himself and all of life are covenantal; and (4) provides a unifying link between biblical and systematic theology, as well as for the various topics in each, since the covenant is central to both and unites the various subordinate topics.

The importance of Kuyper's view of the Trinity cannot be overstated. Without the doctrine of the covenant among the persons of the Trinity, the tendency to abstraction dominates thought about God, and there is no basis for a real link between God as He is in Himself and God as He relates to man. Also, the doctrine of man, both as individual and as related in society, suffers from a neglect of the doctrine of the trinitarian covenant, for to rightly understand man, we must view him as a covenant personality.

Kuyper was not the first Reformed theologian to believe in a covenant among the persons of the Trinity. Already at the time of the Reformation, Olevianus saw the doctrine of salvation as rooted in a trinitarian covenant.

> In the broader context in which the *sponsio* language occurs, Olevianus considers the promise of the Son as part of a wider pretemporal redemptive agreement between the Father and the Son, but only once does he actually call the agreement a covenant (*pactum*). In this arrangement the Father gives the Son a command, the Son promises to obey it, and the Father then accepts the Son's obedience. [3]

Heinrich Heppe gives evidence from Heidegger, Burman, Witsius, Cocceius, Cloppenburg and Voetius that Reformed theologians held to what he calls a "Trinitarian pact." He explains,

---

[3] Lyle D. Bierma, *German Calvinism in the Confessional Age: The Covenant Theology of Caspar Olevianus* (Grand Rapids: Baker, 1996), 109.

This *pactum* by which the Son, in order to become the mediator of the Father's testament, became its sponsor and the second Adam of the human race, is still not an event in the Trinity first produced temporally through the fall, different from the Father's eternal counsel. On the contrary it is essentially connected with the fallen human race and yet is an element in the eternal and unalterable decree of God Himself.[4]

Mastright is quoted as follows:

The Reformed recognize both that God most freely demanded that the Son should take up the province of mediator, and that the Son had undertaken it with equal freedom, in that each acted on rational design and assent
. . . .[5]

Even Charles Hodge, whose view of the covenant of redemption is primarily soteriological, writes:

By this [covenant of redemption] is meant the covenant between the Father and the Son in reference to the salvation of man. This is a subject which, from its nature, is entirely beyond our comprehension. We must receive the teachings of the Scriptures in relation to it without presuming to penetrate the mystery which naturally belongs to it. There is only one God, one divine Being, to whom all the attributes of divinity belong. But in the Godhead there are three persons, the same in substance, and equal in power and glory. It lies in the nature of personality, that one person is objective to another. If, therefore, the Father and the Son are distinct persons the one may be the object of the acts of the other. The

---

[4] Heinrich Heppe, *Reformed Dogmatics: Set Out and Illustrated from the Sources*, ed. Ernst Bizer, trans. G. T. Thomson (1950; reprint, Grand Rapids: Baker, 1978), 378.
[5] Ibid., 379.

one may love, address, and commune with the other. The Father may send the Son, may give Him a work to do, and promise Him a recompense. All this is indeed incomprehensible to us, but being clearly taught in Scripture, it must enter into the Christian's faith.[6]

Kuyper, however, expresses the trinitarian significance of the covenant more fully than any of his predecessors.

If the idea of the covenant with regard to man and among men can only occur in its ectypical form, and if its archetypical original is found in the divine economy, then it cannot have its deepest ground in the *pactum salutis* that has its motive in the fall of man. For in that case it would not belong to the divine economy as such, but would be introduced in it rather incidentally and change the essential relations of the Three Persons in the divine Essence. Besides, the objection arises that the Third Person of the Holy Trinity in that case remains outside of this covenant and that the Three Persons in the eternal Essence are placed in such a relation over against one another that one runs the danger of falling into the error of tritheism. This danger can be escaped only when the divine economy of the Three Persons is presented *natura sua* as a covenant relation. . . . We then confess that in the one personality of the divine Essence there consists a three-personal distinction, which has in the covenant relation its unity and an inseparable tie. God Himself is, according to this conception, not only of every covenant, but of the covenant idea as such the living and eternal foundation; and the essential unity [of the Godhead] has in the covenant relation its conscious

---

[6] Hodge, *Systematic Theology*, 2:359–60. Note that the various statements Hodge makes about the persons of the Trinity illustrate what Plantinga wrote about Augustine's doctrine, that on the one hand he believes in the scriptural doctrine of the three persons, but on the other hand they reduce in the end to one.

expression. Father, Son, and Holy Ghost stand accordingly over against all what is not God or what opposes God in that unity of faithfulness that the one does not will anything else than the other, and the entire power of the divine Essence turns itself with the highest consciousness in federal unity against all that is not God.

And when in this manner the foundation of the covenant idea is found in the confession of the Trinity itself, then follows from this the further covenant relation between the Father, Son, and Holy Spirit which is determined by the appearance of ungodliness in the world of angels and men, not only according to the idea of its possibility, but according to the idea of its reality. For when we proceed from the confession of the Trinity to the confession of the decree, then the reality of it is a matter of fact, and the federal unity in God must be directed to the complete conquest of the fact of sin, in order that God may be triumphant. And this leads to the *constitutio Mediatoris*, not as an act of force, but as a federal action, and thus arises the *pactum salutis*. In the covenant relation Father, Son, and Holy Spirit aim together and each for Himself at the triumph over sin, that is, at the triumph over all that which places itself over against God as anti-God. The ground of this will in God is found in the original covenant relation in the divine Essence; and that which is to be accomplished by the Father, the Son, and the Holy Spirit respectively unto that end continues to find its federal unity in the *opus exeuns* which is common to the Three Persons. That which is assumed as the work of the Father, the Son, and the Holy Spirit respectively does not rest on arbitrary division of labor, but on the distinction which exists between Father, Son, and Holy Spirit in the divine Essence itself, and that not only in the world of salvation, but also already in the work of creation. Hence, the *pactum salutis* can never include only the two, but must always include the Three Persons of the Holy Trinity. Besides, considering that the decree

knows not of two possibilities, with or without sin, but
only of the reality, that is, the reality of sin, this *pactum*
does not appear after the fall, but recedes into eternity
and forms the point of procedure of the entire *pactum
salutis*. And when the *pactum salutis* thus stands behind
the fall and has its root in the *decretum*, it follows *eo ipso*
that the introduction of it started immediately after the
fall, and that a suspension of it until the hour of the in-
carnation is inconceivable.[7]

As Kuyper says, unless the covenant relationship is seen to
be an aspect of the interpersonal relationships of the Father,
the Son, and the Spirit, there is no way of accounting for the
persons of the Godhead entering into a covenant to redeem
man. Nor is there any way to account for the fact that creation itself and God's relationship with man both before and
after redemption is always covenantal. Even heaven is de-
scribed in John's Revelation as the place where the covenant
will be fulfilled forever (Rev. 21:1–3; etc.).

The argument here is theological rather than exegetical,
but we must not think of Kuyper constructing the doctrine
of the ontological Trinity out of philosophical concerns and
then deducing a theoretical paradigm that is forced onto
Scripture. While he insists that the ontological Trinity must
be the ultimate ground for the doctrine of the covenant, his
starting point is the fact of God's covenantal work of redemption in history.[8] We may say, then, that Kuyper's view
expresses the principle made famous by Karl Rahner in his

---

[7] Qtd. in Herman Hoeksema, *Reformed Dogmatics*, 295–96.

[8] Kuyper's argument in the quotation above answers John H. Stek's demand
that the idea of the centrality of the covenant be given adequate theological justification. Stek believes that Reformed theology suffers from "covenant overload."
He critiques various views of the covenant in recent authors such as Meredith
Kline, *By Oath Consigned* (Grand Rapids: Eerdmans, 1968); O. Palmer Robertson,
Christ of the Covenants (Grand Rapids: Baker, 1980); William J. Dumbrell, *Covenant and Creation: A Theology of Old Testament Covenants* (Nashville: Thomas

notion of the axiomatic unity of the economic and immanent Trinity: "The 'economic' Trinity is the 'immanent' Trinity and the 'immanent' Trinity is the 'economic' Trinity." Rahner formulates the principle in bold language that invites distortion, but the idea itself is not new. Herman Bavinck phrases this traditional notion more carefully when he writes: "The ontological trinity is reflected in the economical trinity."[9]

Following the Reformed tradition in general and Kuyper in particular, we must emphasize the covenant relationship among the Father, the Son, and the Spirit. God is a covenantal God because He is the triune God of love. Both Plantinga's social view of the Trinity and Van Til's emphasis on the persons need the doctrine of the covenant to develop their most replete biblical forms.

Nelson, 1984); and Thomas E. McComiskey, *Covenants of Promise: A Theology of the Old Testament Covenants* (Grand Rapids: Baker, 1985). However, not only is his critique based upon a theologically defective view of the covenant, he also misses some of the most important details in the views that he criticizes. For example, Dumbrell's view of the Noahic covenant, which is carefully and fully argued, is dismissed for being supposedly built upon the use in Genesis 6:18 and 9:9,11 of the verb קוּם with בְּרִית rather than the verb כרת. But Stek completely overlooks the most decisive literary evidence to which Dumbrell appeals, the repetition of the exact language of Genesis 1:28, etc., in Genesis 9:1–3. See "Covenant Overload in Reformed Theology," *Calvin Theological Journal* 29, no. 1 (1994): 23–24.

[9] Herman Bavinck, *The Doctrine of God* (Edinburgh: Banner of Truth Trust, 1977),317–18. Bavinck's work was first published in Dutch near the end of the nineteenth century. In context Bavinck's quote is: "Now these inter-personal relations existing within the divine essence are also revealed outwardly. To be sure, outgoing works always pertain to the Divine Being as a whole. 'God's outgoing works are indivisible although the order and distinction of the persons is preserved.' One and the same God reveals himself in creation and redemption. But in this unity the order of subsistence within the divine essence is preserved. The ontological trinity is reflected in the economical trinity. Hence, certain attributes and works are ascribed particularly—though not exclusively, as was held by Abelard—to one person, others especially to another, in such a manner that the order of subsistence pertaining to the ontological trinity is revealed in this outward manifestation."

Covenantal Language and God's Attributes

Van Til notes the relationship between the doctrine of the Trinity and the doctrine of the attributes of God:

> In other words, we are bound to maintain the identity of the attributes of God with the being of God in order to avoid the specter of brute fact. In a similar manner we have noted how theologians insist that each of the persons of the Godhead is co-terminous with the being of the Godhead. But all this is not to say that the distinctions of the attributes are merely nominal. Nor is it to say that the distinctions of the persons are merely nominal. We need both the absolute cotermineity of each attribute and each person with the whole being of God, and the genuine significance of the distinctions of the attributes and the persons.[10]

Though he demands a real distinction in the attributes, Van Til does not go on to relate the attributes to the doctrine of the Trinity. It appears that Van Til affirms a basically Augustinian view of the simplicity of God, but he unequivocally denies that God's simplicity may be taken to imply that plurality in God's attributes or personhood is not real or is less important. Van Til's view suggests revision may be necessary, but Plantinga's social view of the Trinity clearly demands a reconsideration of the doctrine of the attributes of God.

The importance of rethinking the doctrine of God's attributes is most clearly seen when we consider perfections of the divine nature like love. These are necessarily not only

---

[10] *IST*, 229. For Van Til, the doctrine of God's simplicity is an aspect of the doctrine of the unity of God. I think that it is fair to summarize his point as follows. When we confess that God is one, we acknowledge that there is a sense in which we must say that God is simple. When we confess that God is three, we are also saying that God is not simply simple. Cf. *IST*, 215–219.

personal qualities, but attributes that require interpersonal relationships. Thus, the doctrine of God's attributes is vitally related to our understanding of the persons of the Trinity. However, in the history of Reformed theology it is common to discuss the attributes of God as if the topic was independent of and prior to the doctrine of the Trinity.[11] The order of discussion in texts of systematic theology usually begins with the doctrine of the one God, including topics like His knowability, His Being, and His nature and attributes. Only after we learn who God is do we learn—by the way, as it were—that He is also triune. Of course, Reformed theologians do not intend to slight the doctrine of the Trinity, but the order of discussion suggests a lower view of the Trinity than they intend. And as a matter of fact, the attributes of God are usually discussed as if there were no trinitarian implications.

This is the procedure followed by virtually all the well-known Reformed theologians from Francis Turretin to Robert L. Reymond, including Charles Hodge, A. A. Hodge, R. L. Dabney, and L. Berkhof. The general presupposition is that the attributes of God are qualities of His essence. The Reformed tradition is basically unified on this. "God's essential attributes," writes Polan, "are really His very essence; and they do not actually differ from God's essence or from each other. Not from the essence; they are in the essence in such wise as to be the essence. Not from each other; whatever there is in God is one. Moreover there ought to be absent from the prime unity all difference and all number whatsoever. In God there is nothing which is not either essence or person."[12]

---

[11] I do not mean to suggest that this is a distinctive of Reformed theology. On the contrary, it has been the common approach at least since the Middle Ages.

[12] Qtd. in Heppe, *Reformed Dogmatics: Set Out and Illustrated from the Sources,* 57–58. Heppe also quotes Mastright saying that divine attributes, "if you mean the fact, are nothing but the one, infinite, perfection of God, according as it is

William G. T. Shedd, unique among eminent Reformed theologians of the nineteenth century in introducing the doctrine of the Trinity before his discussion of the attributes of God, explains the difference between a person and an attribute. "The difference between a Divine attribute and a Divine Person is, that the person is a mode of the existence of the essence; while the attribute is a mode either of the relation, or of the external operation of the essence. The qualifying adjective 'external' is important; because the internal operation of the essence describes a trinitarian person. When the Divine essence energizes *ad intra*, the operation is generation, or spiration, and the essence so energizing is the Father, or the Son; but when the Divine essence energizes *ad extra*, the operation is omnipotence, or omniscience, or benevolence, etc. A trinitarian person is a mode of the essence; a divine attribute is a phase of the essence."[13]

It is clear from Shedd's explanation that the attributes qualify the essence of God, which the persons of the Trinity share. For each of the persons is the whole essence of God. In that sense, then, discussion of the attributes is seen as an aspect of the doctrine of God's essence. Apart from the fact that the persons of the Trinity share that essence, the attributes have been considered to be unrelated to the doctrine of the Trinity per se. Furthermore, Shedd suggests that attributes like love refer to "external operations of the essence." If this is true, intratrinitarian love is ruled out by definition.

---

apprehended by us in various inadequate concepts. To our so-called formal concepts, really differentiated from each other, there answer on God's side various objective concepts, the note of which in God is but one infinite perfection, apprehensible by our understanding, owing to its native finitude and weakness, only in various acts, in parts as it were" (60). It may be noted that Robert Lewis Dabney objected vehemently to this kind of language. Robert L. Dabney, *Lectures in Systematic Theology* (Grand Rapids: Zondervan, 1972), 148.

[13] William G. T. Shedd, *Dogmatic Theology* (reprint, Minneapolis: Klock & Klock, 1979), 1:335–36.

Traditional Reformed theology, in other words, appears to presuppose something close to the very notion Van Til objects to: the idea that the essence of God is an impersonal substratum. As a matter of fact, traditional Reformed theology has been significantly influenced by the Aristotelian and medieval idea of "substance" in formulating the doctrine of the Trinity. Needless to say, this influence is not limited to Reformed theology; it is the mainstream church tradition. But it is not the only approach. As far back as Athanasius, the notion of God's essence was defined apart from Aristotelian notions of substance.

The Reformed tradition is also complex. For example, although he did not fully develop the idea he introduced, Herman Bavinck did at least suggest a trinitarian approach to understanding the attributes of God.

> The Eternal Being reveals Himself in His triune existence even more richly and vitally than in His attributes. It is in this holy Trinity that each attribute of His Being comes into its own, so to speak, gets its fullest content, and takes on its profoundest meaning. It is only when we contemplate this Trinity that we know who and what God is. Only then do we know, moreover, who God is and what He is for lost mankind. We can know this only when we know and confess Him as the Triune God of the Covenant, as Father, Son, and Holy Spirit.[14]

[14] Herman Bavinck, *Our Reasonable Faith: A Survey of Christian Doctrine* (Grand Rapids: Baker, 1977), 143. Bavinck does not go on to explain how the doctrine of the Trinity relates to the attributes of God or to the covenant. Nor does he, in his later discussion of the covenant, develop this point further, but treats the covenant of redemption as God's eternal counsel to save sinners. All the same, the statement here testifies eloquently to the centrality of the Trinity in our knowledge of God and the need for a comprehensive application of the Trinity to the Christian worldview. Karl Barth also implied the need for a trinitarian approach to the attributes of God, both in the order of his discussion, beginning with the Trinity, and in specific statements about the attributes

The scope of the present chapter prohibits a full consideration of the biblical description of God's attributes, but the following introductory discussion suggests that the biblical language confirms Bavinck's statement, "It is in this holy Trinity that each attribute of His Being comes into its own, so to speak, gets its fullest content, and takes on its profoundest meaning."

With Bavinck in mind, we will consider briefly three attributes, love, righteousness, and faithfulness, each of which points to God as covenantal in His essential nature. In other words, these attributes find their meaning only in the context of interpersonal relationships. If words describing the attributes of God require for their understanding both the notion of the covenant and interpersonal relationships, it is reasonable to conclude that at least some of God's attributes describe first of all the covenantal relationship of the persons of the Trinity.

LOVE

The attribute of love is the most obviously trinitarian. Traditional Reformed theology has usually subsumed the notion of love under that of God's goodness. This is not altogether wrong, for goodness is another word that points to the covenantal nature of the love of God. In one of the most important passages in the Old Testament, God promises Moses, "I will make all my goodness pass before thee" which is explained to mean, "I will proclaim the name of the LORD before thee" (Exod. 33:19). Goodness is, thus, a broad description of who God is, and like other aspects of God's nature, is associated with the covenant idea.[15] Passages like

---

of God. However, since he has reduced the persons of the Trinity to something less than "subjects" in the interest of preventing tritheism, he cannot expound the real meaning of the Trinity and the attributes of God.

[15] Cf. Delbert R. Hillers, *Covenant: The History of a Biblical Idea* (Baltimore: Johns Hopkins Press, 1969), 113. Note the use of the word *goodness* in association

Jeremiah 33:11 are especially relevant here: ". . . Give thanks
to Jehovah of hosts, for Jehovah is good, for His lovingkindness
[חֶסֶד / hesed] endureth for ever . . . ." God's goodness is
manifested in His generous bestowal of the gifts and blessings
of the covenant, for which we owe Him praise and worship.
The goodness of God is the active expression of His love and

---

with other covenant terms in Isaiah 63:7. "I will mention the lovingkindnesses
[חֶסֶד] of the LORD, and the praises of the LORD, according to all that the LORD
hath bestowed on us, and the great goodness toward the house of Israel, which
he hath bestowed on them according to his mercies [רַחֲם], and according to
the multitude of his lovingkindnesses [חֶסֶד]." For other uses of *goodness* with
חֶסֶד, see Judg. 8:35; 2 Sam. 2:6; Jer. 33:11; Mic. 6:8; Ps. 23:6; 25:7; 63:3;
69:16; 86:5; 100:5; 106:1; 107:1; 109:21; 118:1; 118:29; 136:1; Prov. 14:22;
19:22; Esth. 2:9; Ezra 3:11; 1 Chr. 16:34; 2 Chr. 5:13; 7:3. Goodness is associated with the name of God in many passages, too: Ps. 25:8; 34:9; 52:9; 54:6;
73:1; 86:5; 119:68; 135:3; 145:9; Lam. 3:25; 2 Chr. 30:18; cf. Nah. 1:7.

Calvin, in his comments on Daniel 9:4, notes the relationship between the
ideas of God's covenant loyalty, grace, and goodness: "He does not put these
two words as differing from each other, בְרִית, *berith*, and חֶסֶד, *chesed*, but
unites them together, and the sentence ought to be understood by a common
figure of speech, implying that God made a gratuitous covenant which flows
from the fountain of his pity. What, therefore, is this agreement or covenant
and pity of God? The covenant flows from God's mercy; it does not spring
from either the worthiness or the merits of men; it has its cause, and stability,
and effect, and completion solely in the grace of God. We must notice this, because those who are not well versed in the Scriptures may ask why Daniel distinguishes mercy from covenant, as if there existed a mutual stipulation when
God enters into covenant with man, and thus God's covenant would depend
simply on man's obedience. This question is solved when we understand the
form of expression here used, as this kind of phrase is frequent in the Scriptures. For whenever God's covenant is mentioned, his clemency, or goodness,
or inclination to love is also added. Daniel therefore confesses, in the first
place, the gratuitous nature of the covenant of God with Israel, asserting it to
have no other cause or origin than the gratuitous goodness of God. He next
testifies to God's faithfulness, for he never violates his agreement nor departs
from it, as in many other places God's truth and faithfulness are united with
his clemency. (Psalm 36:6, and elsewhere.) It is necessary for us to rely on
God's mere goodness, as our salvation rests entirely with him, and thus we
render to him the glory due to his pity, and thus it becomes needful for us, in
the second place, to obtain a clear apprehension of God's clemency. The language of the Prophet expresses both these points, when he shows how God's
covenant both depends upon and flows from his grace, and also when he adds
the Almighty's faithfulness in keeping his agreement."

hesed.[16] So are God's jealousy and His wrath. It is because God is the God who loves and gives Himself in love that He is also a jealous God who will not tolerate a violation of the covenant.[17]

Modern discussions of the attributes of God, rather than subsuming love under goodness, tend to view love as God's primary attribute. Millard J. Erickson regards an understanding of love as a key to understanding the Trinity, asserting that, "The Trinity is three persons so closely bound together [by love] that they are actually one."[18] Stanley Grenz, too, apparently following Pannenberg, regards love as the attribute of God which most clearly reveals His nature.[19] While I regard it as mistaken to make one attribute "fundamental," it is certainly the case that the biblical statement "God is love" requires the notion of interpersonal relationships in God.

What is left out, however, by those asserting the primacy of love is the biblical meaning of love. Love, like goodness, requires the associated idea of the covenant in order to correctly expound its biblical meaning.[20] Consider, for example, the book of Hosea, which most emphatically declares God's love for Israel. When the prophet proclaims that God's love for His people is analogous to the prophet's love for a wayward woman, it is clear that God's love for His people is "emotional" in some sense of the word, as well as covenantal.

---

[16] See the following discussion on God's faithfulness for an explanation of *hesed*.

[17] See H. G. L. Peels, *New International Dictionary of Old Testament Theology and Exegesis* (Grand Rapids: Zondervan, 1997), s.v. "קנא" (5:938–39).

[18] Erickson, *God in Three Persons*, 221.

[19] Grenz, *Theology for the Community of God* (Nashville: Broadman and Holman, 1994), 92–93.

[20] This is not to say that the words for love are always used in a specifically covenantal sense. For a discussion of the various Hebrew and Greek terms and their usage, see Leon Morris, *Testaments of Love: A Study of Love in the Bible* (Grand Rapids: Eerdmans, 1981), 8ff., 101ff.

But the "emotional" aspect of God's love is expressed in the gift of the covenant relationship. God betroths Israel to Himself in love, righteousness, and faithfulness.[21] In Hosea, love means the establishment of a covenantal relationship through the marriage oath. This view of God's love for His people is grounded in the covenant love declared in Deuteronomy.[22] Because love means mutual commitment, self-sacrifice, and giving, there is a whole range of terms associated with the word *love* that show it clearly to be a covenantal idea.[23]

God's love to His people is manifested first of all in His gracious bestowal of the covenant upon the fathers (Deut. 10:15), and it continues to be seen in His faithfulness to Israel (cf. Deut. 23:5; 1 Kgs. 10:9; 2 Chr. 2:11; 9:8; 20:7; Is. 61:8; Hos. 3:1; Mal. 1:2; Ps. 11:7; 33:5; 37:28; 87:2; 146:8; Prov. 3:12; 15:9). Jeremiah declares: "The LORD hath appeared of old unto me, saying, Yea, I have loved [אָהַב / *ahab*] thee with an everlasting love: therefore with lovingkindness [*hesed*] have I drawn thee" (31:3).[24]

The covenantal character of the biblical idea of love is especially seen in the nature of the love that is demanded of God's covenant people as the essence of their response to His love:

Love in Deuteronomy is a love that can be commanded. It is also a love intimately related to fear and reverence. Above all, it is a love which must be expressed in loyalty,

---

[21] See the discussion in Francis I. Anderson and David Noel Freedman, *Hosea*, vol. 24 of *The Anchor Bible* (New York: Doubleday, 1980), 282–84.

[22] Hans Walter Wolff, *Hosea: A Commentary on the Book of the Prophet Hosea* (Philadelphia: Fortress Press, 1978), 59–61.

[23] Some of those words are: *jealous* (Deut. 6:4–15; Zech. 8:1–17), *faithful* (Deut. 7:6–16), *bless* (Deut. 7:6–16, esp. 7:13), *oath* (Deut. 7:6–16, esp. 7:8), *fear / obedience* (Deut. 10:12; 11:13; 30:20), *commandments* (Exod. 20:6; Deut. 5:10, 7:9; 11:1, 13, 22; 30:16).

[24] *Love* [אָהַב] is often used with חֶסֶד: Exod. 20:6; Deut. 5:10; 7:9; Jer. 31:3; Mic. 6:8; Ps. 33:5; 119:159; Esth. 2:17; Dan. 9:4; Neh. 1:5.

in service, and in unqualified obedience to the demands of the Law. For to love God is, in answer to a unique claim (6,4), to be loyal to him (11,1.22; 30,20), to walk in his ways (10,12; 11,22; 19,9; 30,16), to keep his commandments (10,12; 11,1.22; 19,9), to do them (11,22; 19,9), to heed them or his voice (11,13; 30,16), to serve him (10,12; 11,1.13). It is, in brief, a love defined by and pledged in the covenant—a covenant love.[25]

In the New Testament, the doctrine of God's love comes to fuller expression, for only with the coming of Christ do we learn how great is God's love for us and of the truth of the triune nature of God Himself. In the New Testament, we are not only told that God gave us His Son because He loved us (Jn. 3:16; Rom. 8:28–36), that He gave us His Spirit because He loved us (Rom. 5:5), and that Jesus loved us and therefore gave Himself (Gal. 2:20; Eph. 5:2), but we are also told that our redemption is grounded in the fact that the Father loves the Son and therefore shows and gives Him all things (Jn. 3:35; 5:20; 17:23–26). This love between Father and Son is clearly an aspect of the trinitarian personal relationship from all eternity: "for You loved Me before the foundation of the world" (Jn. 17:24). Therefore, any treatise on theology proper which does not include the intertrinitarian love of the Father, Son, and Spirit misses what is most essential and wonderful.

FAITHFULNESS

Closely related to the word *love*, but also including the notion of faithfulness or loyalty, is the Hebrew word חֶסֶד (*hesed*), which occurs 247 times in the Hebrew text of the

---

[25] William L. Moran, "The Ancient Near Eastern Background of the Love of God in Deuteronomy," *The Catholic Biblical Quarterly* 25 (1963): 78. The verse references uses a nonstandard style; e.g., 6,4 = 6:4; 11,1.22 = 11:1, 22.

Old Testament[26] and is translated variously as mercy (Gen.
19:19, KJV), kindness (Gen. 21:23, KJV), goodness (Exod.
34:6, KJV), lovingkindness (Exod. 34:6, ASV, NASB), stead-
fast love (Exod. 34:6, RSV, NRSV), and love (Exod. 34:6,
NIV). Nelson Glueck's famous study of *hesed* demonstrated
that it and its synonyms are used in the Bible as distinctly
covenantal terms. According to Glueck, *hesed* is the "premise
and effect" of a covenant and is said even to constitute "the
very essence" of a covenant, though it is not precisely synonymous with the word *covenant*. Writing of *hesed* as a divine
attribute, Glueck says,

> In different contexts חֶסֶד can be translated differently
> as "faithfulness," "assistance," "covenant," or "love." All
> these are aspects of the total concept. For example, חֶסֶד
> is not some kind of arbitrary assistance, but rather that
> which the members of a covenant are obligated to prac-
> tice reciprocally. This meaning of חֶסֶד as the faithful,
> mutual assistance among people who are bound together
> by a covenantal relationship mirrors, perhaps, the origi-
> nal meaning of the word.[27]

---

[26] Francis Brown, S. R. Driver, and Charles Briggs, *A Hebrew and English Lexicon of
the Old Testament* (Oxford: The Clarendon Press, 1972), 338. Leon Morris gives the
number 245 times in *Testaments of Love,* 65. He also notes the difficulty of translating
the word and the various attempts.

[27] *Hesed in the Bible,* 82. If we think in terms of a covenant relationship among the
persons of the Trinity, the original meaning of the word will be "a faithful mutual assistance among persons who are eternally bound by covenant." Moshe Weinfeld not
only concurs with Glueck's findings, he demonstrates that the Greeks and Romans
borrowed treaty terminology from the East. He concludes that "The identity in covenant formulations and idiomatic expressions in Mesopotamia, Syro-Palestine,
Anatolia, Greece, and Rome seems to point towards a common origin of the treaty
terminology in the ancient world." See "Covenant Terminology in the Ancient Near
East and Its Influence on the West," *Journal of the American Oriental Society* 93 (no. 2,
1973): 197. The parallels between biblical terms and those of the ancient near east in
general are particularly evident in the use of the word *love* in ancient Egyptian,
Sumerian, Akkadian, and Aramaic documents. See Jan Bergman and A. O. Haldar, s.v.
"אָהַב" in *Theological Dictionary of the Old Testament*, ed. by G. Johannes Botterweck and
Helmer Tingren (Grand Rapids: Eerdmans, 1974), 1:99–101.

Although scholars like Glueck see *hesed* as first of all a term that conveys the idea of "good relationship," which is later used as a technical term in treaties, I believe the movement must have been in the other direction, from the covenantal use to the more general.[28] From a Christian perspective, it is certain that God's covenants with Adam and Noah, and perhaps also later covenants with Abraham and Moses, are the source for the widespread occurrence of the covenantal idea and covenantal language in the ancient world.[29] Also, however the analogous word groups may be used in other languages, I am inclined to regard the use of *hesed* in the Bible as always covenantal, that is, as either explicitly or implicitly alluding to a covenant of some sort. Although awkward in English, I prefer to translate it as "covenant-love," "covenant-kindness," "covenant-loyalty," or "covenant-faithfulness."

When used of God in the Bible, the word חֶסֶד is quite clearly covenantal. God's *hesed* "rests on the בְּרִית [covenant] by which he has freely bound himself to his people . . . ."[30] Thus, " . . . the thought of חֶסֶד and the thought of the covenant belong together."[31] *Hesed*, then, when used of God, points to the fact that He is faithful to His gracious covenant promise because He is a God of love and mercy. Goodness, kindness, love, and mercy all express aspects of what is involved in the idea of *hesed*, but

---

[28] Contrary to Leon Morris, who writes, "It is too much to say that the word originates in the usages of covenant. We can say however, that it is the right word to designate the attitude that the partners of a covenant ought to have toward one another" (*Testaments of Love*, 69). Here is a case where one's doctrine of the Trinity and his lexicography influence one another considerably. If there is an eternal covenantal relationship among the persons of the Godhead, covenantal usage is most profoundly primary.

[29] I am not suggesting a direct relationship, as if people in the ancient world self-consciously borrowed from the biblical idea. I am saying that covenantal ideas were part of the racial heritage passed on through Noah.

[30] Bultmann, s.v. "ἔλεος" in Gerhard Kittel and Gerhard Friedrich, eds. *Theological Dictionary of the New Testament,* trans. G. W. Bromiley, 10 vols. (Grand Rapids: Eerdmans, 1974), 2:479.

[31] Ibid., 480.

what these English translations do not include is the covenantal idea, something that would have not only been obvious, but prominent for the Hebrew reader. In addition, the use of the covenant term *hesed* in parallel with other words describing God's attributes is an important indication of the similar covenantal significance of these other words.

The declaration of the divine name to Moses places special emphasis on God's covenantal kindness and love, repeating the word *hesed* in order to bring out God's covenantal character:

> And Jehovah descended in the cloud, and stood with him there, and proclaimed the name of Jehovah. And Jehovah passed by before him, and proclaimed, Jehovah, Jehovah, a God merciful and gracious, slow to anger, and abundant in lovingkindness [*hesed*] and truth, keeping lovingkindness [*hesed*] for thousands, forgiving iniquity and transgression and sin; and that will by no means clear the guilty, visiting the iniquity of the fathers upon the children, and upon the children's children, upon the third and upon the fourth generation. (Exod. 34:5–7)[32]

Here, then, in one of the most important passages in the biblical teaching about the nature of God, we find both an emphatic repetition of the covenantal attribute *hesed*, and the use of the word truth [אֱמֶת / *emeth*] as a near synonym of it. In fact the two words are used together often and usually translated "mercy and truth."[33] The frequent parallel use of the terms suggests that they are both associated with the covenant idea. *Truth* may indeed be used to refer to that which is

---

[32] Quotation from the American Standard Version.
[33] See Gen. 24:27, 49; 32:10; 47:29; Exod. 34:6; Josh. 2:12, 14; 2 Sam. 2:6; 15:20; 1 Kgs. 3:6; Is. 16:5; Hos. 4:1; Mic. 7:20; Zech. 7:9; Ps. 25:10; 26:3; 40:10–11; 57:3, 10; 61:7; 69:13; 85:10; 86:15; 89:14; 108:4; 115:1; 117:2; 138:2; Prov. 3:3; 14:22; 16:6; 20:28.

the opposite of falsehood,[34] but it is most commonly used to mean something like "faithfulness," or "reliability." When used of God, the word suggests not only His truth in the sense that He "cannot lie," but also that because He cannot lie and is thus true to His covenant oath and promise, He is the God who is to be relied upon.

The idea of faithfulness is so closely associated with love that the word *hesed* includes both. To Israel God proclaims Himself as the faithful God, and His faithfulness is seen as both the ground for blessing and cursing: "Therefore know that the LORD your God, He is God, the faithful God who keeps covenant and mercy for a thousand generations with those who love Him and keep His commandments; and He repays those who hate Him to their face, to destroy them. He will not be slack with him who hates Him; He will repay him to his face" (Deut. 7:9–10).

Even as the idea of faithfulness is close to the notion of love, it is also close to the idea of righteousness: "Righteousness shall be the belt of His loins, and faithfulness the belt of His waist" (Is. 11:5).[35] God's faithfulness endures to all generations (Ps. 119:90; cf. Deut. 7:9). Therefore, we can rely without fear on His promises (1 Cor. 1:9; 1 Thes. 5:24; 2 Thes. 3:3; Heb. 11:11). For God to be other than faithful would be self-denial (2 Tim. 2:13).

---

[34] For example, as in Deuteronomy 13:14, "Then shalt thou inquire, and make search, and ask diligently; and, behold, if it be truth, and the thing certain, that such abomination is wrought among you. . . ." Cf. also Deut. 17:4; 22:20.

[35] See also Is. 59:4; Jer. 5:1; Ps. 40:10; 96:13; 119:138; etc. Note that the Hebrew word often translated "faithful" (אמונה) is also translated "truth" in some cases.

Righteousness

Righteousness is another attribute of God associated with the covenant idea.[36] Just as a man's righteousness is defined in terms of the covenant commandments,[37] God's righteousness is understood by the covenant law and by His bestowing the blessings and curses of the covenant according to true judgment (Hos. 14:9; Ps. 7:1–11; 11:5–7; 14:5; 18:20–27; 37:1–40; 48:8–10; 55:22; 58:11; 85:9–15; 89:14; 96:13; 112:4; 116:5; 119:75, 138, 142, 172; 145:17; 146:8; Lam. 1:18; Dan. 9:14). As Walther Eichrodt points out,

> One expression of Yahweh's covenant love is his righteousness. Just as the חֶסֶד which God desires from man includes the practice of righteousness—for a correct attitude toward the rights of others is at any rate one important aspect of willingness to take one's part in community—so God shows his favour by doing justice and righteousness.[38]

He goes on to explain that God's righteousness "is his keeping of the law in accordance with the terms of the covenant."[39] Eichrodt refers to H. Cremer's "insight of genius" in describing righteousness as "a concept of relation referring

---

[36] Again this word is used with חֶסֶד in important passages: Is. 16:5; 57:1; Hos. 2:19; 10:12; Ps. 85:10; 89:14.

[37] Cf. Ezekiel 18:9, "Hath walked in my statutes, and hath kept my judgments, to deal truly [literally, "to do חֶסֶד"]; he is just, he shall surely live, saith the Lord GOD." Here it is clear that the idea of a righteous man is a covenantal idea. He is the man who "does חֶסֶד" and keeps the commandments of God. Cf. Ezek. 3:20ff.; 18:5, 20ff. See also Exod. 15:26; Deut. 6:18; 12:28; 13:18; 1 Kgs. 11:38; 14:8; 15:5; Neh. 9:13; Ps. 19:8; 119:128,137; Hos. 14:9. There are many too passages in the Old Testament which associate righteousness with keeping the commandments of God to doubt that this is a basic idea.

[38] Walther Eichrodt, *Theology of the Old Testament*, 1:239–40.

[39] Ibid. As the context following this quotation reveals, there are serious problems in Eichrodt's notion of the covenant and the idea of righteousness. He is, nevertheless, correct in seeing that the two notions are inseparable.

to an actual relationship between two persons and implying behaviour which corresponds to, or is true to, the claims arising out of such a relationship."[40]

The idea is that when a man is true to the claims of the covenant by obedience to God, he is righteous. On man's side, the commandments of God are the claims of the covenant specified. But we must add that a man who kept the precepts of the law without loving God would not be righteous. He would certainly not be a criminal either, and may well be thought righteous. But he would not be righteous because love is essential to the righteousness of the law, since the first and greatest commandment is to love God and the second greatest commandment is to love your neighbor. If the whole law hangs on these two commands, then righteousness requires love.[41]

On God's side, righteousness is associated with just judgment. He curses those who ought to be cursed according to the covenant law and He blesses those who ought to be blessed. That is to say that God keeps His covenant promises. His faithfulness to the covenant is His righteousness.

Herman Bavinck observes[42] that God's righteousness is "synonymous with lovingkindness" (hesed),[43] that the "manifestation of God's righteousness is at the same time the showing forth of his grace,"[44] and that even "the forgiveness of sins is due to God's righteousness."[45] He concludes,

---

[40] *Theology of the Old Testament*, 1:240.

[41] Note that in Deuteronomy righteousness is used as virtually synonymous with "uprightness of heart" in 9:5 and is the opposite of "stiff-necked" in 9:6.

[42] The following quotations from Bavinck all come from *The Doctrine of God* (Edinburgh: Banner of Truth Trust, 1977), 218.

[43] Bavinck offers the following Scripture references: Ps. 22:31; 33:5; 35:28; 40:10; 51:15; 89:14; 145:7; Is. 45:21; Jer. 9:24; Hos. 2:18; Zech. 9:9. Note that given the covenantal meaning of *hesed*, Bavinck's statement here conflicts with his denial that righteousness means "covenant faithfulness."

[44] Ibid.: Ps. 97:11–12; 112:4; 116:5; 119:15–19.

[45] Ibid.: Ps. 51:15; 103:17; 1 Jn. 1:9.

"Hence, the revelations of that righteousness are deeds of re-demption, deeds of salvation and deliverance."[46]

Bavinck adds the following to his statements above:

> Although in this manner righteousness and salvation are brought into very close relation to each other, it is nevertheless incorrect to regard them as synonyms. Righteousness is not identical with favor, compassion, grace; neither does it mean covenant-faithfulness (Diestel, Ritschl, Kautzsch, and others); nor is salvation the negative side, and righteousness the positive, as Davidson would have it. Righteousness is always a forensic concept; but in the O. T. the most important task and the strongest evidence of righteousness is the protection of the oppressed, and the deliverance of the needy from the injustice and persecution to which they are subjected. That was the content of God's righteousness; hence, this execution of judgment on behalf of the needy became the primary task of the earthly king and judge.[47]

If the emphasis in Bavinck's statement falls on the word "identical" when he says that "righteousness is not identical with favor," etc., we can agree with Bavinck's point here. But the fact remains that the biblical notion of righteousness does not make sense as a forensic term in the abstract. The universe is not ultimately impersonal. Nor are there impersonal principles or "laws" which govern the world or man. The notion of law in the Bible, and therefore, also, the idea of righteousness, is inescapably a matter of interpersonal relationships, which is why it is possible for Jesus to summarize the law in terms of love. Also, if righteousness is to have any meaning in the interpersonal relationships of the persons of the Trinity, it cannot be limited to forensic ideas

---

[46] Ibid.: Judg. 5:11; 1 Sam. 12:7; Ps. 103:6; Is. 45:24–25; Mic. 6:5.
[47] Ibid., 219.

or to the notion of obedience to commandments. Rather than strictly legal notions, the following sort of interpersonal ideas must be prominent: faithfulness to the covenant, an inflexible commitment to bless the beloved, the integrity that is associated with covenantal loyalty.

It is with the concreteness of covenantal relationship in mind that The New Testament scholar N. T. Wright says, "The church appropriated for itself the Jewish belief that the creator god [*sic*] would rescue his people at the last, and interpreted that rescue in terms of a great law-court scene. This is the doctrine of the 'righteousness of God', the *dikaiosune theou*, which is best seen in terms of the divine covenant faithfulness, and which comes to major expression in Paul's letter to Rome."[48] Justification is not the declaration that we are regarded as having conformed to abstract principles or a contractual demand. Justification is the declaration that God accepts us as righteous in Christ. He receives us as His beloved people.[49]

Bavinck also warns that the dogmatic view of righteousness was not always the same as the biblical. This does not mean that the use of the word "righteousness" in dogmatic theology as "the constant and perpetual desire to grant to every individual his due" is necessarily wrong. It does mean that

---

[48] *The New Testament and the People of God* (Minneapolis: Fortress Press, 1992), 458. I am not entirely comfortable with Wright's discussion of justification, but I do believe he is correct in taking the position that forensic categories are covenantal and relational. Nothing can be impersonal in a world created by the triune God. If law is the way of love, then justification is not judicial in any abstract contractual manner, which is the way the older reformed notion of the covenant of works is sometimes applied.

[49] Jesus Himself, in His action and teaching, illustrates the personal and covenantal nature of biblical righteousness. The parable of the prodigal son is a good example of both aspects united. To begin with, the occasion for the parable was the fact that the Pharisees and scribes were offended that Jesus was eating with sinners. That Jesus should do such a thing contradicted their notions of righteousness and proved that He must be a false prophet. But for Luke, Jesus' action was actually a demonstration of His righteousness, and the

care must be taken to put the dogmatic use into the context of the biblical idea of the covenant. Bavinck concludes that while it is wholly impossible for the creature to have any inherent claim to reward, because God has established His covenant with man, He is "obliged to save his people and punish the wicked."[50]

Righteousness is based in the covenant. While it does not seem appropriate to see righteousness as simply "synonymous" with faithfulness, it must be closely related to faithfulness, as also to love. For the attributes of God are all related; each expounds the other. And since they are all attributes of the triune God, no attribute can be impersonal.

TRINITARIAN IMPLICATIONS

These are not by any means the only covenantal terms used to describe the attributes of God, but this brief survey does indicate something of the biblical basis for our statement that at least some of the attributes of God must be understood as covenantal. If the words used in the Bible to describe God's attributes are covenantal terms and if we take God's revelation of Himself in the economy as a true revelation of who He is, then we may infer from this covenantal language that there is a covenantal relationship among the persons of the Trinity and that it is ultimately in that everlasting covenantal relationship that words like love, covenant loyalty or faithfulness, and righteousness have their meaning.

---

parable that Jesus told to the Pharisees explained His actions. The older brother protests at his father's celebration over the prodigal's return, reminding his father, "for these many years I have served you and I never transgressed your commandment" (Luke 15:29). He is righteous in the way the Pharisees were righteous, a defective righteousness that missed the real issue. How can the son be truly righteous when he is so far from the heart of his father that he cannot rejoice with him? By contrast, the father's love for his wayward son is true righteousness.

[50] See Bavinck's extended treatment in *The Doctrine of God*, 221–223.

Consider what this means when we try to understand God's love. Love in God is single, insofar as each of the attributes of God is coterminous with His essence, but it is hard to imagine what that would mean if love were not also an attribute describing the covenantal relationship of the Father, the Son, and the Spirit. Each of the persons loves the other. This means that they give themselves to one another with the full self-sacrificial offering that God displayed when He loved us and gave His Son for us. Love is giving. Furthermore, we must also assume that the Father and Son share in their love for the Spirit, the Father and the Spirit share in their love for the Son, the Son and the Spirit share in their love for the Father. When we say that God is love, we mean much more than what can be expressed by asserting that each of the attributes of God is coterminous with His essence. In the doctrine of the covenantal relationship among the three persons of the Trinity we find the biblical ground for Plantinga's statement, "The Trinity is thus a zestful, wondrous community of divine light, love, joy, mutuality, and verve."[51]

God's faithfulness is the total commitment of each of the persons of the Trinity to the covenant relationship among them, the absolute commitment of each to the other two. Each person of the Trinity is faithful to the oath implicit in the covenant relationship.

Van Til defines the righteousness of God as "internal self-consistency." He explains that God is "absolute law," which means that God cannot and does not tolerate any subordination of any one aspect of his being to any other aspect of his being."[52] This approach to defining God's righteousness may sound abstract compared to a trinitarian approach, but there

---

[51] "TOPT," 50.
[52] *IST* (Philipsburg, N.J.: Presbyterian and Reformed, 1974), 245.

is no disparity. Righteousness means that each of the persons of the Trinity is wholly dedicated to preserving the properties of the others. They never transgress the boundaries of their personhood but rather act to protect them by blessing and glorifying one another. They uphold the law-covenant of their triune being, the essence of which is love.

When we think of the attributes in terms of the covenant, love, faithfulness and righteousness are distinguishable but mutually interpenetrating perfections. None is conceivable without the others. Love that did not maintain the boundaries of the covenant would not be love, even as faithfulness or righteousness without love would be devoid of meaning.

Slightly revising Bavinck, we may say that it is in the covenantal relationship of the persons of the holy Trinity that each attribute of His Being comes into its own, so to speak, gets its fullest content, and takes on its profoundest meaning. It is only when we contemplate the persons of the Trinity in covenant that we know who and what God is. Love, faithfulness, and righteousness are first of all terms that describe the relationships among the persons of the Trinity.

DIRECTION FOR REFORMATION

Covenant theology, according to John Murray, "marked an epoch in the appreciation and understanding of the progressiveness of divine revelation."[53] This is true not only of the later, more fully developed covenant theology of the seventeenth century—even in Calvin's *Institutes*, the doctrine of the covenant provides a basis for understanding the unity and progressive development of revelation.[54] Its contribution to the doctrine of revelation together with its contribution to

---

[53] John Murray, *The Covenant of Grace* (reprint, Philipsburg, N.J.: Presbyterian and Reformed, 1988), 3.
[54] Ibid., 3–4.

the doctrine of salvation accounts for the great impact of covenant theology in the history of the Church. As great, however, as these contributions are, Murray felt that covenant theology needed to be recast, and he warned against the idea that "covenant theology is in all respects definitive and that there is no further need for correction, modification, and expansion." "Theology," Murray reminds us, "must always be undergoing reformation."[55] Murray suggests that covenant theology needs to refine or correct its definition of the covenant.

The reformation of the doctrine of the covenant that Murray sought, however, had been clearly stated already by Kuyper.[56] Though the idea of a covenant among the persons of the Trinity has neither been included in Reformed confessions nor was ever universally held,[57] it remains true that from the time of the Reformation, the idea that Father, Son, and Spirit entered into a covenant to redeem fallen man has been an important part of the Reformed theological tradition. Kuyper rightly insisted that a covenant to redeem fallen man cannot be the beginning of the covenant relationship among the persons, for it would imply a change in God. Also, the biblical language describing God's attributes implies that we can only understand God rightly when we consider the covenantal fellowship of love in the Trinity. The doctrine of a covenant among the persons of the Trinity may be the most

---

[55] Ibid., 4–5.

[56] I know that Murray would have disagreed.

[57] See, for example, Geerhardus Vos, "The Doctrine of the Covenant in Reformed Theology" in Richard B. Gaffin, Jr. ed., *Redemptive History and Biblical Interpretation: The Shorter Writings of Geerhardus Vos* (Philipsburg, N.J.: Presbyterian and Reformed, 1980), 234ff. See also Lyle D. Bierma, *German Calvinism in the Confessional Age: The Covenant Theology of Caspar Olevianus* (Grand Rapids: Baker, 1996); and Charles S. McCoy and J. Wayne Baker, *Fountainhead of Federalism: Heinrich Bullinger and the Covenantal Tradition* (Louisville, Ky.: Westminster/John Knox Press, 1991).

important single "theological" contribution of Reformed Christianity, for the following reasons:

1. The doctrine shows us more of what it means that God is fully personal and illumines the biblical teaching that God is love in terms of the persons of the Trinity being freely committed to one another in an everlasting bond.

2. Although a covenant is not necessarily a document and it does not have to be altogether spelled out, it is a relationship that can be defined by words. That God is a God of language is suggested by the fact that Christ, the eternal Word, is "with God"—a covenantal expression—from eternity.

3. It is essential to a covenant between persons that they freely enter the relationship, especially a covenant of love. The freedom of the persons of the Godhead is expressed in their utter self-commitment to one another in the everlasting covenant of love.

4. A covenant is also law. Freedom, love, and law are all essential to the full understanding of a covenant. They meet in the covenant notion in a sort of perichoretic fashion, each expounding the other.

5. For us, the doctrine of a covenant among the persons of the Trinity places worship and obedience at the center of the Christian life. Knowledge, science, business, family, and all the other concerns of life in this world are within the sphere of our covenant relationship with God. The covenant is entered officially by baptism and is renewed by the Lord's Supper. Only in worship, when we bow down before Him in thanksgiving and praise, have we adopted the proper epistemological posture.

6. The Christian worldview, biblical theology, and systematic theology all take the triune God Himself as their

center. Whereas "theism" in the abstract does not include the trinitarian covenant which is the ultimate explanation for all, the foundation for the Christian "theory of everything," a biblically developed trinitarianism points the way to a systematic theology in which every doctrine is related to God through the covenant idea—creation is the establishment of the covenantal kingdom; sin is covenantal rebellion; redemption is covenantal restoration; eschatology is the realization of the covenant in history and eternity. Biblical theology describes the development of the covenant in the history of God's dealings with man, beginning with the covenant in the Garden, which was renewed with Noah, Abraham, Moses, David, and the restored exiles, and which was at last fulfilled wholly in Christ, the last Adam. The Christian worldview must be designed to show how the triune God covenantally relates to history, art, literature, and other academic disciplines.

Returning to Plantinga and Van Til, either of their formulations of the Trinity is consistent with the notion of a covenantal relationship among the persons of the Godhead. But neither of them picks up Kuyper's teaching or works to reconstruct the doctrine of the Trinity in specifically Reformed terms. For that is just what Kuyper's doctrine does. It distinguishes Reformed theology from all other theological traditions in its doctrine of the Trinity. If Kuyper is correct, as I believe he is, the covenant among the persons of the Trinity must be the starting point for our theological and intellectual endeavor. This requires a revision of Reformed theology and Reformed academics in terms of the knowledge of the triune God.

Conclusion

Karl Rahner's famous complaint about the neglect of the doctrine of the Trinity, seconded by Moltmann, no longer applies to nonevangelical circles where the situation has drastically changed. While there remain serious problems with the orthodoxy of some recent views of the Trinity, there is in any case nothing like neglect. Thomas R. Thompson calls it a "Trinitarian Renaissance."[1] Among evangelicals, however, a revival of interest in the doctrine of the Trinity, which should have occurred long before it did among liberals, has yet to happen—in spite of the fact that both Abraham Kuyper and Cornelius Van Til proffered significant revisions of the doctrine of the Trinity which could have been central to the twentieth century conflict between the Christian and non-Christian worldviews, or at least been the source of serious discussion among evangelical Christians of all sorts. For some reason, the contributions of Kuyper and Van Til have been overlooked, even by Carl F. H. Henry, who was theologically competent enough to understand the far-reaching import of their ideas. A small group of Reformed thinkers have attempted to apply their views more broadly, but there is not yet among evangelicals anything that might truly be called a

---

[1] "Trinitarianism Today: Doctrinal Renaissance, Ethical Relevance, Social Redolence," *Calvin Theological Journal* 32 (no. 1, April 1997): 10.

"renaissance" in the doctrine of the Trinity, though there is a growing interest provoked by nonevangelical scholars.

This is not the way it ought to be. The doctrine of the Trinity is the very beating heart of the Christian system of truth. We must not only confess our trinitarian faith with joy, we must so live that the triune God Himself is the center of all. If evangelicals do not know how to think and teach to this end, we confront what must be the greatest theological and practical problem for evangelical faith.[2]

To revive interest and stimulate discussion, someone must stir the waters. Van Til did, but few people were willing to join the conversation. It seems clear that Van Tillians need to remind the broader evangelical world of Van Til's contributions and encourage the kind of discussion and debate that can help bring about reformation. I believe that Van Til offers evangelicals foundational insights (1) in the way he expounds the Trinity as a mystery, (2) in his application of the doctrine of the Trinity to the problem of the one and the many, and (3) in the social implications of his trinitarianism, understood in the light of Kuyper's view of the covenant.

First, the doctrine of the Trinity is a mystery and Van Til was correct for emphasizing the paradoxical nature not only of this but of all truth. It is hard to imagine anyone putting the point in more perplexing terms than Van Til's: "God is a one consciousness being, and yet he is also a tri-conscious being."[3] While the social trinitarians seek to reduce the notion of mystery as much as possible, we have seen, or at least argued, that they raise as many problems as they solve. It is

---

[2] Millard Erickson's *God in Three Persons* illustrates the weakness in evangelicalism. What Erickson does discuss is relatively well done. The problem with his book is what he ignores. Even if he were not acquainted with Kuyper's covenantal views, how could he be ignorant of Van Til's discussion of the Trinity as it relates to the problem of the one and the many? If he will not interact with Van Til, why not Gunton?

[3] *IST*, 220.

simply not true, as Thompson suggests, that a doctrine of the Trinity as "mystery"—meaning beyond human comprehension—necessarily means that the Trinity is an "opaque" doctrine which will not "readily make for an acute ethical vision."[4] No theologian has offered a more concrete ethical vision than that suggested by Van Til[5] and elaborated by Vern Poythress.[6] Van Til's view of the mystery of the Trinity requires an epistemology that is revelational and, we may add, liturgical. In Van Til's theology the fact that God is a Trinity means that the Scriptures themselves must be the standard for all thought, and that we truly know God or His word in the worshipful faith of covenantal confession. Certainly an incomprehensible mystery is "opaque" in one sense. But in the Van Tillian approach the mysterious nature of the Trinity forces one to subject his thought more carefully to the Scriptures so that he may discover that harmony of the one and the many in daily life, which can never be known apart from God's revelation.

It should also be added that "mystery" does not mean "irrational." Van Til argues for a rational view of the world, but insists that the ultimate rationality of God is beyond human comprehension. Reason in man is not given as an ultimate judge of the truth but a tool to be employed in a spirit of humble faith and worship. The biblical doctrines of the triune

---

[4] "Trinitarianism Today," 9.

[5] "It will be considered extravagant to say that men will not regard anything as authoritative that has not emanated from themselves. It is important to note, though, that it has been Kant who has given the idea of autonomy its modern form, and who has most effectively spread this idea that it was after all involved in the very bedrock of all non-theistic ethics. The ethics of Plato and Aristotle are autonomous, as well as the ethics of Kant. There is no alternative but that of theonomy and autonomy. It was vain to attempt to flee from God and flee to a universe in order to seek eternal law there." Van Til, *Christian Theistic Ethics* (Philipsburg, N.J.: Presbyterian and Reformed, 1980), 134. Emphasis in original.

[6] *The Shadow of Christ in the Law of Moses* (Brentwood, Tenn.: Wolgemuth and Hyatt, 1991).

God and man's covenant with Him do not call Christians to subscribe to irrationalism any more than to yield to autonomous reason.

Second, I suspect that most Van Tillians will be inclined to agree with the social trinitarians' critique of Augustine for his overemphasis on the oneness of God. But this does not require an entire rejection of Augustine's views or even the analogy that he offers. Perhaps this is another way of saying that a Van Tillian critique of Augustine differs from that of a social trinitarian like Thompson, who charges the Western tradition with teaching a doctrine that is unimaginable and which, therefore, stifles imagination. "One can imagine God as either one person or three. To frame a picture of God as both one and three persons at the same time appears impossible—a veritable law of noncontrapiction if a neologism be permitted."[7]

Van Til's notion that the doctrine of the Trinity is the biblical solution to the philosophical problem of the one and the many connotes something very different. If the doctrine of the Trinity is the biblical solution to the problem of the one and the many, then everything in the world which reflects the problem of the one and the many is an illustration of the doctrine of the Trinity. Since all created reality reflects the problem in some form, Van Til's view is certainly not restraining the human imagination by incomprehensible notions. It is a call for much broader analogical thinking and, I believe, also an invitation to reconsider the whole biblical-symbolic picture of the world.[8]

What this means for Augustine's doctrine is that the problem is not so much what he said, but what he did not say. He presented a lopsided view of the Trinity because his analogy

---

[7] "Trinitarianism Today," 41.

[8] See James Jordan, *Through New Eyes: Developing a Biblical View of the World* (Brentwood, Tenn.: Wolgemuth & Hyatt, 1988).

was a oneness analogy without a corresponding threeness
analogy or, to put it in different terms, he failed to see that
everything in the world which reflects the problem of the one
and the many is an analogy of the Trinity. Rather than reject
Augustine's analogy, what we need to do is add to it other
analogies. As Thompson says, we cannot hold all of these
analogies in mind at the same time, but that is true of the biblical symbolism of the Messiah also. We can picture Him as
the Lamb of God and we can picture Him as the Lion of the
tribe of Judah, but not both at the same time.[9] Were
Thompson's "law of non-contrapiction" accepted as valid, it
would erase much of biblical symbolism.

Assuming that Van Til is correct in concluding that the
Trinity is the biblical solution to the one and the many implies
not only that everything which reflects that problem—all of
created reality—in one way or another includes some
reflection of the Trinity, it also may be said to imply that there
are at least two different kinds of analogies, oneness analogies
and threeness analogies.[10] For example, considering the
doctrine of the Trinity in terms of the biblical picture of the
Father "generating" the Son and the Father and Son together
"spirating" the Spirit is a picture of the one unfolding into
three, a picture that social trinitarians conspicuously under-
emphasize. On the other hand, the covenantal analogy begins
with three persons who come together in one in a covenantal
commitment of love, a picture of the three uniting into one.

---

[9] This is true of many if not all biblical symbols. Israel is God's bride, but
Jerusalem is His daughter. And the Bride is a priestly nation, though women
cannot be priests. The Church is Christ's body and bride at the same time. In
short, biblical symbolic language is not meant to be reducible into one picture.
God gives us multiple pictures because the truth is so complex and many-fac-
eted. We do not err when we take them one at a time, so long as we don't
absolutize any particular picture.

[10] Poythress offers examples of analogies that express the threefold
personhood of God.

Neither of these pictures alone is adequate, but together they teach us of a God who is equally one and three—neither one before three nor three before one. Does our inability to put the whole picture together neatly mean that we cannot picture aspects of the truth profitably?

It may help here to compare the situation we have in the doctrine of the Trinity to another subject. Consider the calendar. The cycles of the day, the month, and the year simply do not fit and there is no way around it. We cannot change the hours of the day to perfectly fit the cycle of the moon and bring them both into harmony with the cycle of the year. God has created the cycles of time in a manner that may seem to us less than neatly arranged. But this has not by any means stifled human imagination. We reconcile ourselves to the fact that the sun and moon do not move according to our mathematical notions of neatness, and imagine an infinite abundance of analogies, pictures, and stories. Van Til's doctrine of the Trinity liberates us from the Augustinian narrowness without taking us to the other extreme and leaving us only with the social analogy. We need both kinds of analogy.

Third, this means that Van Tillians can indeed take advantage of the insights of the social trinitarians. It is important, however, to add to the social trinitarian view two important doctrines that rescue it from merely vague relevance. Kuyper's exposition of the Trinity as a specifically covenantal society tells us more precisely what kind of implications are contained in the social view of the Trinity. Van Til's view that only by obedience to the revealed word of Scripture can we actually realize the harmony of the one and the many in human society renders the notion of covenantal society fully concrete. God's commandments are the standard for the harmony of the one and the many. Worship and obedience, not perfect intellectual comprehension, are the key to covenantal blessing.

The covenant in God is the ground for the existence of the covenant in creation and the key for our understanding the whole world as a covenantal system. Obviously, man's relationship to God Himself and men's relationships to one another are also covenantal. The Bible as the covenantal standard of truth is therefore the key to all knowledge, which is just another way of saying that all the treasures of wisdom and knowledge are hidden in Jesus Christ (Col. 2:3). The covenantal links among the persons of the Godhead, between God and the world, between man and man, and between man and the creation denote a worldview that is anything but opaque.

Fourth, it is profoundly significant that Van Til brought prayer into the debate about the Trinity, for it is in worship that Christian people learn how to think about God. Prosper of Aquitaine is said to have coined this axiom: *legem credendi lex statuat supplicandi* ("the law of prayer found the law of belief").[11] If Christians pray to God as one without always being conscious of the trinitarian persons, and also commonly address their prayers to the Father, in the name of the Son, and by the power of the Spirit, they will naturally think of God along Van Tillian lines, even if they are not adept at expressing themselves theoretically. They will think of God as "one person" in a certain manner of speaking, and they will also more properly think of God as three persons. As a matter of fact, this is the way that most Christians pray and think. Though Van Til's expression is paradoxical, it is, perhaps paradoxically, also closer to the faith of the common Christian man and his manner of prayer. Of course, if Van Til's view is in error, traditional

---

[11] Catherine Mowry Lacugna, *God for Us: The Trinity and the Christian Life* (San Francisco: HarperCollins, 1991), 112. Her chapter on "Living the Trinitarian Faith" is a good example of the poverty of practical trinitarianism among those who do not understand that the Trinity drives us to the Scriptures for wisdom to work out the harmony of the one and the many in daily life.

forms of prayer must be changed in order to correct the "practical Van Tillianism" of the man in the pew. In either case, reformation of worship in the direction of more self-consciously trinitarian forms is necessary, for it is in the weekly worship of God that God's people are going to express their faith in praise and prayer. What we do in worship directs the way think and live. Van Til's view hints at the need for the development of what we might call "liturgical epistemology."

In Van Til's doctrine, we have the basis for an evangelical renaissance of trinitarianism that is at once a call to faith, worship, and obedience to the triune God and also a call to concretely apply God's covenantal Word to all of life. We have a liturgical epistemology that rejoices in the mystery of the triune God while it also enjoins a biblical ethic. Van Til, in other words, answers the casuistry of Kant's famous complaint:

> The doctrine of the Trinity, taken literally, has *no practical relevance at all,* even if we think we understand it; and it is even more clearly irrelevant if we realize that it transcends all our concepts.[12]

What could be more relevant than a doctrine that answers Kant's quest for a concrete transcendental ground for human knowledge? What could be more practical than a doctrine of the Trinity as a covenantal society that calls men to covenantal worship and obedience? The real offense here is that the doctrine of the Trinity demands that we relinquish our pretended autonomy and bow the knee to God.

For too many evangelicals, the doctrine of the Trinity has been tamed, locked up in the cage of a confession of faith that is rarely reflected upon. Kant's words are not altogether inapplicable to this sort of trinitarianism. Van Til's doctrine,

---

[12] Quoted in Thompson, "Trinitarianism Today," 9. Emphasis in original.

by contrast, is more relevant than Kant or his followers can handle. Released from the cage of mere tradition without relinquishing the truth of the tradition, Van Til's approach is dangerous for the world of unbelief, which is happy when the Christian worship of God is confined to pretty buildings. Covenantal trinitarianism implies the kind of "biblicism" that offends the world because it proclaims salvation in Christ alone and offends the Church because it demands reformation. The alternative to a real reformation of evangelicalism in the direction of a fully trinitarian worldview can, I fear, only be apostasy, for the Trinity is the Christian doctrine of God, without which Christianity itself cannot be. But our doctrine of God must be both expressible in a comprehensive worldview system, and also able to inspire worship and obedience in everyday life.

Appendix A
From *On the Trinity*
by Hilary of Poitiers

The following passage is excerpted from Book Five of *On the Trinity*.[1]

1. Our reply, in the previous books, to the mad and blasphemous doctrines of the heretics has led us with open eyes into the difficulty that our readers incur an equal danger whether we refute our opponents, or whether we forbear. For while unbelief with boisterous irreverence was thrusting upon us the unity of God, a unity which devout and reasonable faith cannot deny, the scrupulous soul was caught in the dilemma that, whether it asserted or denied the proposition, the danger of blasphemy was equally incurred. *To human logic it may seem ridiculous and irrational* to say that it can be impious to assert, and impious to deny, the same doctrine, since what it is godly to maintain it must be godless to dispute; if it serve a good purpose to demolish a statement, it may seem folly to dream that good can come from supporting it. *But human logic is fallacy in the presence of the counsels of God, and folly when it would cope with the wisdom of heaven; its thoughts are fettered by its limitations, its philosophy confined by the feebleness of natural reason.* It must be foolish in its own eyes before it can be wise unto God; that is, it must learn the poverty of its own faculties and seek after Divine wisdom. *It must become wise, not by*

[1] From the "Church History Collection" (CD-ROM) published by Galaxie Software.

the standard of human philosophy, but of that which mounts to God, before it can enter into His wisdom, and its eyes be opened to the folly of the world. *The heretics have ingeniously contrived that this folly, which passes for wisdom, shall be their engine.* They employ the confession of One God, for which they appeal to the witness of the Law and the Gospels in the words, Hear, O Israel, the Lord thy God is One. They are well aware of the risks involved, whether their assertion be met by contradiction or passed over in silence; and, whichever happens, they see an opening to promote their heresy. If sacred truth, pressed with a blasphemous intent, be met by silence, that silence is construed as consent; as a confession that, because God is One, therefore His Son is not God, and God abides in eternal solitude. If, on the other hand, the heresy involved in their bold argument be met by contradiction, this opposition is branded as a departure from the true Gospel faith, which states in precise terms the unity of God, or else they cast in the opponent's teeth that he has fallen into the contrary heresy, which allows but one Person of Father and of Son. Such is the deadly artifice, wearing the aspect of an attractive innocence, which the world's wisdom, which is folly with God, has forged to beguile us in this first article of their faith, which we can neither confess nor deny without risk of blasphemy. We walk between dangers on either hand; the unity of God may force us into a denial of the Godhead of His Son, or, if we confess that the Father is God and the Son is God, we may be driven into the heresy of interpreting the unity of Father and of Son in the Sabellian sense. Thus their device of insisting upon the One God would either shut out the Second Person from the Godhead, or destroy the Unity by admitting Him as a second God, or else make the unity merely nominal. For unity, they would plead, excludes a Second; the existence of a Second is destructive of unity; and Two cannot be One.

2. But we who have attained this wisdom of God, which is folly to the world, and purpose, by means of the sound and saving profession of true faith in the Lord, to unmask the snake-like treachery of their teaching; we have so laid out the plan of our undertaking as to gain a vantage ground for the display of the truth without entangling ourselves in the dangers of heretical assertion. We carefully avoid either extreme; not denying that God is One, yet setting forth distinctly, on the evidence of the Lawgiver who proclaims the unity of God, the truth that there is God and God. We teach that it is by no confusion of the Two that God is One; we do not rend Him in pieces by preaching a plurality of Gods, nor yet do we profess a distinction only in name. But we present Him as God and God, postponing at present for fuller discussion hereafter the question of the Divine unity. For the Gospels tell us that Moses taught the truth when he proclaimed that God is One; and Moses by his proclamation of One God confirms the lesson of the Gospels, which tell of God and God. *Thus we do not contradict our authorities, but base our teaching upon them, proving that the revelation to Israel of the unity of God gives no sanction to the refusal of Divinity to the Son of God; since he who is our authority for asserting that there is One God is our authority also for confessing the Godhead of His Son.*[2]

---

[2] Emphasis added. It is important to note that Hilary was trained in philosophy and skillfully employed logic in the arrangement of his thesis and the refutation of his opponents.

Appendix B
Lee Irons on Van Til

Among those who are critical of Van Til's doctrine of the Trinity, Lee Irons's essay on the internet[1] is at least gracious in the sense that Irons does not call Van Til a heretic or attack him personally. However, he does believe that Van Til's doctrine of the Trinity sounds unorthodox, that Van Til relies upon idealistic philosophical categories to the detriment of scriptural accuracy, that Van Til's epistemology has led him to confusion in the doctrine of the Trinity, and that his doctrine is dangerously misleading. Lee charges that Van Til's view implies modalism.

What becomes clear to the reader of Irons's essay is that Irons has a relatively slim grasp of what Van Til is saying, insofar as he misunderstands Van Til's terminology at a number of crucial points, and that his critique of Van Til is not burdened with a broader understanding of the history of the doctrine of the Trinity or the sources to which Van Til frequently alludes. Irons has obviously read more carefully than some of Van Til's critics, but he has not by any means taken the time to do the work necessary for an internal critique of Van Til's thought, which is what he claims to be attempting in his essay. Nor has he done adequate study of the doctrine of the Trinity and its history, with the result that the reader cannot trust his judgment

[1] "Van Til's Philosophical Misuse of the Trinity," <http://members.aol.com/ironslee/private/VTtrinity.htm>.

on particular points and, indeed, it is sometimes doubtful if
Irons himself understands what he is saying.

One of the best examples of Irons's apparent ignorance of
the doctrine of the Trinity in Western history is to be found in
his notion of subordinationism. It is rather difficult to state
exactly what in Irons's thinking the word *subordinationism*
should denote. He seems to think that the Nicene Creed was
subordinationist, for he writes, "It should now be clear that
the orthodox, Nicene doctrine of the eternal generation of
the Son, with its subordinationist implications, is quite un-
suitable for Van Til's philosophical agenda." In Irons's view,
then, *subordinationism* is a word that describes an aspect of the
orthodox doctrine of the Trinity.[2]

In traditional Western theological usage, however, the
word usually connotes something definitely erroneous.
Michael O'Carroll, for example, explains subordinationism
as a "theory about the Trinity which sees the Son as in some
way less than or inferior to the Father, or the Holy Spirit as
subordinate to both."[3] O'Carroll explains that it is common
to charge the theologians of the second and third centuries
with the subordinationist "error," but he clearly prefers to see
the ante-Nicene writers as underdeveloped rather than tend-
ing toward heretical opinions. It is, however, nonetheless true
that the tendency of subordinationist thinking came to its

---

[2] In fairness to Irons, it may be pointed out that he is not the only one who
uses the word "subordination" in this manner. A. A. Hodge asks what "kind of
subordination" the early writers spoke of and answers his own question by ex-
plaining that the persons are equal in essence, but that there is a "relative subordination" with respect to personal subsistence and order of operation (*Outlines of
Theology*, 193). Cf. also Charles Hodge, *Systematic Theology*, 1:474. It is more
common in Trinitarian discourse to use the word subordination to refer to the
Arian position that the Son is inferior to the Father in essence.

[3] Michael O'Carroll, *Trinitas: A Theological Encyclopedia of the Holy Trinity*
(Collegeville, Minn.: The Liturgical Press, 1987), 207. See also the extended
discussion of the Arian controversy in R. P. C. Hanson, *The Search for the Christian Doctrine of God* (Edinburgh: T & T Clark, 1988).

fullest expression in Arius, who asserted in no uncertain terms that the Son and the Spirit were ontologically inferior to the Father. O'Carroll also holds to the common judgment that the Nicene Creed eliminated subordinationism:

> A conclusion that the Son came of a voluntary decision of the Father to help him in creating and ruling the universe would be heresy. The substance of the Father and the substance of the Son, the Council of Nicaea would affirm, are one. This identity precludes any possibility of the Son depending on an act of the Father's will.[4]

Thomas F. Torrance, too, expresses the traditional view on the subject when he labels "Arianism, subordinationism, and Sabellianism" as "damaging heresies."[5] Reformed philosopher Gordon Clark, in a passage correcting what he regards as a mistake in Hodge, writes, "This seems to be an historical mistake because the Nicene Creed excludes every kind of subordination of essence. It states the absolute unity of the divine being or essence."[6]

Contrary to Nicene orthodoxy, which attempted to exclude the possibility of any sort of subordinationism by the assertion that the Father and the Son were of the same essence, Irons sees the notion of the eternal generation of the Son as implying "subordinationism." I assume that Irons intends to use the term in a manner consistent with Nicene orthodoxy, but I am not quite sure what he really means, nor am I altogether certain that he knows precisely what he intends by the term.

A similar sort of confusion reigns in Irons's discussion of Van Til's idea that the persons of the Trinity are "mutually

---

[4] Ibid.

[5] Thomas F. Torrance, *The Christian Doctrine of God: One Being, Three Persons* (Edinburgh: T & T Clark, 1996), 115.

[6] Gordon Clark, *The Trinity* (Jefferson, Md.: Trinity Foundation, 1985), 113.

exhaustive" of one another. Irons writes,

> Especially problematic is Van Til's assertion that each of
> the three persons of the Godhead is equally and fully ex-
> haustive of the being of God. ". . . The persons of the
> Godhead are mutually exhaustive of one another, and
> therefore of the essence of the Godhead" (IST, 220). Note
> the radical nature of this assertion. "Exhaustive" is the
> operative term here. Each person entirely exhausts the
> other two persons. And the entire divine essence is ex-
> hausted by each person. According to Van Til the three
> persons of the Godhead are no more independently ex-
> isting hypostases than are the attributes of God. . . . [7]
>
> If it is true that each of the persons of the Trinity is
> mutually exhaustive of the others, then it would seem
> logically to follow that the traditional appeal to the dis-
> tinction between person and substance is no longer
> valid.

What does he understand by Van Til's language? What does
he think the traditional doctrine is? The reader who takes the
time to check Van Til's sources and try to understand what he
means will discover that Van Til is using nontraditional language to express the traditional idea of "perichoresis," explained more fully above in chapter 3. To say that each of the
persons "exhausts" the others is simply to say that the Father,
Son, and Spirit indwell one another wholly and perfectly. In
this mutual indwelling, the three are one in a manner that
transcends our comprehension. Nothing in the Father is hidden from the Son or from the Spirit, because in their mutual
indwelling each of the persons is wholly transparent to the
other two. Within the fellowship of the Godhead, there is no
mystery. This does not, however, entail that the Son or the

---

[7] Does anyone in the history of the Christian Church regard the three persons as "independently existing hypostases"? This phrase goes further in the direction of tritheism than the language of social trinitarians.

Spirit absorbs that which is the distinct property of the Father or vice versa. Nor is there anything in the ancient doctrine of perichoresis that has ever been thought to imply that the distinction between person and substance is eliminated if each person indwells the other, which is what Van Til means when he speaks of the persons "exhausting" one another.

If Irons intended to criticize the traditional doctrine of the Trinity either for its obscurity or for its tendency to overemphasize the oneness of God, as Plantinga does, it might have been easier to follow what he was trying to say. As it is, he seems to be as confused about what Van Til wrote as he is about the traditional doctrine, and the reader becomes confused about exactly what doctrine of the Trinity Mr. Irons wishes to advocate.

One of his main contentions is that, contrary to Van Til's frequently repeated and argued doctrine of the equal ultimacy of the one and the many in the triune God, Van Til does not really hold to the equal ultimacy of the one and the many, but that the "unity within the Godhead is fundamental and that the plurality exists in perfect systematic coherence with that unity." For Van Til, Irons says, unity has priority over plurality. If Irons could prove that Van Til has indeed overemphasized the unity of God— and it is as highly doubtful that he can prove it as it is obvious that he has yet to do so—then he would be offering a corrective to Van Til, not a refutation. For whether or not Van Til was successful in maintaining the equal ultimacy of the one and the many in the way that he explained the doctrine of God, it was surely his intention to do so. If Irons demonstrated that he failed, it would be a call for revision, not rejection.

There is much more in this essay that seems misguided, but it would be tedious to deal with it in detail, and until Irons takes the time to understand the history of the doctrine of the Trinity and the doctrine of Van Til that he is trying to critique, there is little need to say more.

Appendix C
John Frame on Van Til

John Frame[1] was the first theologian to call attention to Van Til's formulation "one person, three persons," and he assumes partial responsibility for the "furor" that arose in response.[2] In particular, Gordon Clark and his disciple, John Robbins, took offense at Van Til's formulation, but not a few others have found it troublesome. Frame shows, however, that common misgivings about Van Til rest in misunderstanding.

He offers four points in reply to critics. First, he reminds readers that Van Til does not regard the Trinity or any other Christian doctrine as a real contradiction. Van Til carefully distinguishes between what appears to be contradictory to us and what is truly contradictory. Admittedly, this means that we ourselves cannot tell the difference between what is contradictory and what is only apparently contradictory unless God Himself reveals the difference to us. But that is just the point. He has revealed Himself and the truth we need to know, both in His Word and in general revelation. With the Scriptures as our standard, we can discern truth and apply it

[1] In the previous chapters I neglected to mention John Frame, not because I consider what he had to say as unimportant but because I agreed with him.

[2] John Frame, *Cornelius Van Til: An Analysis of His Thought* (Philipsburg, N.J.: Presbyterian and Reformed, 1995), 65–66. The whole of chapter five is a discussion of Van Til's view of the Trinity.

for the realization of the goal of human life, the kingdom of God.

Second, at the end of his first point, Frame points out that Van Til does not deny the traditional view; he is only intending to add that when we speak of God as one in essence and three in person, we must not think of God's essence as an impersonal substratum of divinity. Thus, Van Til is not replacing or denying the traditional view.

What this means is elaborated more fully in Frame's second point where he defends the formula "one person" more fully, claiming that Clark and Robbins have not responded to Van Til's arguments on behalf of that view. Van Til asserted what all orthodox Christians have believed when he wrote that each of the persons of the Trinity is "coterminous with the being of the Godhead." This is just another way of saying that each person is fully God, possessing all the attributes of divinity. As Frame says, Van Til's point is that "God is one being, not three."[3]

Frame explains:

God is not an abstraction. Nor is he a mere society of three gods, united by common abstract properties.

What is he, then? As we indicated earlier, Van Til's answer is that God is an "absolute person." Abstractions are impersonal. God is a concrete, personal reality. Our world is ruled by a person, not an abstract principle. As Van Til says, when God identified himself to us in revelation, "there was no universal being of which he was a particular instance." If the three persons (individually and collectively) exhaust the divine essence (are "coterminous" with it), then the divine essence itself must be personal. And if God is an absolute person, and he is one, there must be a sense in which he is one person.[4]

---

[3] Ibid., 67.
[4] Ibid., 68.

Van Til, in other words, attempts to qualify our understanding of the one being of God to guard from any tendency
toward impersonalism.

Third, how do we relate the one person to the three? This
is a mystery for which there is no answer that can wholly satisfy our minds. What can be pointed out is that since Van Til is
not rejecting, but merely qualifying the traditional formula,
the oneness of God and the threeness of God are not to be
thought of as identical, which would entail a simple contradiction. God is not, therefore, one person in precisely the
same sense that He is three persons.

Frame's fourth point is a consideration of the meanings of
the word "person" in Van Til's formula. Van Til, Frame says,
"obviously" uses the word person in different senses when he
discusses the threeness of God and the oneness of God. But
no precise definition of terms may be offered since to presume to define these notions precisely is to transgress the
limits inherent in creaturehood.

In this connection, Ronald Nash relates an illuminating
personal incident in a discussion of Van Til's thought:

> I once asked Van Til if, when some human being knows
> that 1 plus 1 equals 2, that human being's knowledge is
> identical with God's knowledge. The question, I thought,
> was innocent enough. Van Til's only answer was to smile,
> shrug his shoulders, and declare that the question was
> improper in the sense that it had no answer.[5]

Nash goes on to explain—incorrectly, in my opinion—Van
Til's view. What he should have noted is that Van Til refuses to
define God's knowledge of an object because to do so is to
presume knowledge of God that we do not and could not
have. In the same way, I believe Van Til would have refused to

---

[5] Ronald H. Nash, *The Word of God and the Mind of Man: The Crisis of Revealed
Truth in Contemporary Theology* (Grand Rapids: Zondervan, 1982), 100.

elaborate about precisely how God is one person and three
persons, since it touches the deepest mystery of the Christian
faith.

Frame further comments on the matter of trinitarian terminology:

> But the creedal tradition, too, fails to give a "precise" ac-
> count of the relations between God's "essence" and his
> "persons." The Greek term *ousia,* which was used to des-
> ignate God's essence, was not, in the Greek language,
> precisely differentiated from *hypostasis,* the term used
> for the three persons. The choice of these terms was to
> some extent arbitrary. The church fathers needed a term
> to designate God's unity, and they chose *ousia.* They
> needed a term or God's plurality, and they chose *hyposta-
> sis.* But there was nothing about either term that
> uniquely fitted it for its particular task, over against the
> other. Indeed, the church fathers might have reversed
> them ("one *hypostasis,* three *ousia*") without loss. The
> Latin church in the West spoke of one *substantia,* but *sub-
> stantia* is by etymology and use more interchangeable
> with *hypostasis* than with *ousia.* In English, we can trans-
> late both *hypostasis* and *substantia* as "substance." On that
> account, we can see that in effect the Greeks spoke of
> God as "three substances" and the Latins of "one sub-
> stance." Doubtless these choices of terms caused some
> misunderstanding. But, from our vantage point, we can-
> not regard either formulation as unorthodox.[6]

In another section, Frame discusses the importance of Van
Til's trinitarian views on the one and the many. By relating
the doctrine of the Trinity to the problem of the one and the
many, Van Til places the doctrine of the Trinity at the center of
every theoretical and practical concern. His approach renders
the doctrine of the Trinity universally applicable and relevant,

---

[6] *Cornelius Van Til,* 69–70.

and at the same time calls for men to submit their minds and hearts to God's Word, for we cannot discover the harmony of the one and the many in our daily lives through speculation. Worship and obedience to the commandments of God are more fundamental to knowledge than philosophical specula- tion. When we submit our minds and hearts to the teaching of the Scriptures, we have light on the God-created harmony of the world that enables us to work out in principle the basic problems of life, whether in church, family, or state, to the glory of God.

Bibliography

Anderson, Francis I., and David Noel Freedman. *Hosea*. Vol. 24 of *The Anchor Bible*. New York: Doubleday, 1980.

Barth, Karl. *Church Dogmatics*. Vol. 1. Edinburgh: T & T Clark, 1975.

Bavinck, Herman. *The Doctrine of God*. Edinburgh: Banner of Truth Trust, 1977.

—————. *Our Reasonable Faith: A Survey of Christian Doctrine*. Grand Rapids: Baker, 1977.

Bergman, Jan, and A. O. Haldar. *Theological Dictionary of the Old Testament*. Ed. G. Johannes Botterweck and Helmer Tingren. Grand Rapids: Eerdmans, 1974.

Bierma, Lyle D. *German Calvinism in the Confessional Age: The Covenant Theology of Caspar Olevianus*. Grand Rapids: Baker, 1996.

Bracken, Joseph. *Society and Spirit: A Trinitarian Cosmology*. Selinsgrove, Penn.: Susquehanna Univ. Press, 1991.

Brown, Francis, S. R. Driver, and Charles Briggs. *A Hebrew and English Lexicon of the Old Testament*. Oxford: The Clarendon Press, 1972.

Clark, Gordon. *The Trinity*. Jefferson, Md.: Trinity Foundation, 1985.

DeMar, Gary. *War of the Worldviews: A Christian Defense Manual*. Atlanta: American Vision, 1994.

De Raeymaiker, Lois. *The Philosophy of Being*. St. Louis: B. Herder, 1954.

Dumbrell, William J. *Covenant and Creation: A Theology of Old Testament Covenants*. Nashville: Thomas Nelson, 1984.

Eichrodt, Walther. *Theology of the Old Testament*. Trans. John Baker. London: SCM Press, 1961.

Erickson, Millard J. *God in Three Persons: A Contemporary Interpretation of the Trinity*. Grand Rapids: Baker, 1995.

Frame, John. *Cornelius Van Til: An Analysis of His Thought*. Philipsburg, N.J.: Presbyterian and Reformed, 1995.

Geisler, Norman, and Paul Feinberg. *Introduction to Philosophy: A Christian Perspective*. 1980. Reprint, Grand Rapids: Baker, 1997.

Grenz, Stanley. *Theology for the Community of God*. Nashville: Broadman and Holman, 1994.

Gunton, Colin. *The Promise of Trinitarian Theology*. Edinburgh: T&T Clark, 1991.

————. *The One, the Three and the Many*. Cambridge: Cambridge Univ. Press, 1993.

Hanson, R. P. C. *The Search for the Christian Doctrine of God*. Edinburgh: T & T Clark, 1988.

Henry, Carl F. H. "God Who Stands and Stays, Part One." In vol. 5 of *God, Revelation and Authority*. Waco, Tex.: Word, 1982.

Heppe, Heinrich. *Reformed Dogmatics: Set Out and Illustrated from the Sources*. Ed. Ernst Bizer. Trans. G. T. Thomson. 1950. Reprint, Grand Rapids: Baker, 1978.

Hilary of Poitiers. *On the Trinity*. CD-ROM, Galaxie Software.

Hillers, Delbert R. *Covenant: The History of a Biblical Idea*. Baltimore: Johns Hopkins Press, 1969.

Hodge, Charles H. *Systematic Theology*. Reprint, Grand Rapids: Baker, 1973.

Hoeksema, Herman. *Reformed Dogmatics*. Grand Rapids: Reformed Free Publishing Association, 1966.

Irons, Lee. "Van Til's Philosophical Misuse of the Trinity." <http://members.aol.com/ironslee/private/VTtrinity.htm>.

Jordan, James B. *The Law of the Covenant*. Tyler, Tex.: Institute for Christian Economics, 1984.

————. *Through New Eyes: Developing a Biblical View of the World*. Brentwood, Tenn.: Wolgemuth & Hyatt, 1988.

Kittel, Gerhard, and Gerhard Friedrich, eds. *Theological Dictionary of the New Testament*. Trans. G. W. Bromiley. Vol. 2. Grand Rapids: Eerdmans, 1974.

Kline, Meredith. *By Oath Consigned*. Grand Rapids: Eerdmans, 1968.

Lacugna, Catherine Mowry. *God for Us: The Trinity and the Christian Life*. San Francisco: HarperCollins, 1991.

McComiskey, Thomas E. *Covenants of Promise: A Theology of the Old Testament Covenants*. Grand Rapids: Baker, 1985.

McCoy, Charles S., and J. Wayne Baker, *Fountainhead of Federalism: Heinrich Bullinger and the Covenantal Tradition*. Louisville, Ky.: Westminster/John Knox Press, 1991.

Moltmann, Jurgen. *The Trinity and the Kingdom*. Minneapolis: Fortress Press, 1981.

Moran, William L. "The Ancient Near Eastern Background of the Love of God in Deuteronomy." *The Catholic Biblical Quarterly* 25 (1963).

Morris, Leon. *Testaments of Love: A Study of Love in the Bible*. Grand Rapids: Eerdmans, 1981.

Murray, John. *The Covenant of Grace*. Reprint, Philipsburg, N.J.: Presbyterian and Reformed, 1988.

Nash, Ronald H. *Worldviews in Conflict: Choosing Christianity in a World of Ideas*. Grand Rapids: Zondervan, 1992.

————. *The Word of God and the Mind of Man: The Crisis of Revealed Truth in Contemporary Theology*. Grand Rapids: Zondervan, 1982.

O'Carroll, Michael. *Trinitas: A Theological Encyclopedia of the Holy Trinity*. Collegeville, Minn.: The Liturgical Press, 1987.

Ogbonnaya, A. Okechukwu. *On Communitarian Divinity: An African Interpretation of the Trinity*. New York: Paragon House, 1994.

Pannenberg, Wolfhart. *Systematic Theology*. Trans. Geoffrey W. Bromiley. Vol. 1. Grand Rapids: Eerdmans, 1991.

Peels, H. G. L. *New International Dictionary of Old Testament Theology and Exegesis*. Grand Rapids: Zondervan, 1997.

Plantinga, Cornelius, Jr. "The Threeness/Oneness Problem of the Trinity." *Calvin Theological Journal* 23, no. 1 (April 1988).

Poythress, Vern S. *The Supremacy of God in Interpretation*. Unpublished syllabus.

————. "Reforming Ontology and Logic in the Light of the Trinity." *Westminster Theological Journal* 57, no. 1 (spring 1995).

————. "Mathematics." In *Foundations of Christian Scholarship: Essays in the Van Til Perspective*, ed. Gary North. Vallecito, Calif.: Ross House Books, 1976.

Rahner, Karl. *The Trinity*. Trans. Joseph Donceel. 1970. Reprint, with new introduction by Catherine Mowry Lacugna, New York: Crossroad, 1997.

Reymond, Robert L. *A New Systematic Theology of the Christian Faith*. Nashville: Thomas Nelson, 1998.

Robertson, O. Palmer. *Christ of the Covenants*. Grand Rapids: Baker, 1980.

Robbins, John W. *Cornelius Van Til: The Man and the Myth*. Jefferson, Md.: The Trinity Foundation, 1986.

Schaeffer, Francis. *He Is There and He Is Not Silent*. Wheaton: Tyndale House, 1972.

Segundo, Juan Luis. *A Theology for the Artisan of a New Humanity*. Maryknoll, N.Y.: Orbis, 1973.

Shedd, William G. T. *Dogmatic Theology*. Vol. 1. Reprint, Minneapolis: Klock & Klock, 1979.

Sire, James W. *The Universe Next Door: A Basic Worldview Catalog*. Downers Grove, Ill.: InterVarsity, 1976.

Sproul, R. C. *Lifeviews: Understanding the Ideas that Shape Society Today*. Old Tappen, N.J.: Fleming H. Revel, 1973.

Stek, John H. "Covenant Overload in Reformed Theology." *Calvin Theological Journal* 29, no. 1 (1994).

Thompson, Thomas R. "Trinitarianism Today: Doctrinal Renaissance, Ethical Relevance, Social Redolence." *Calvin Theological Journal* 32, no. 1 (April 1997).

Torrance, Thomas F. *The Christian Doctrine of God: One Being, Three Persons*. Edinburgh: T & T Clark, 1996.

Turretin, Francis. *Institutes of Elenctic Theology*. Philipsburg, N.J.: Presbyterian and Reformed, 1992.

Van Til, Cornelius. *The New Modernism*. Philadelphia: Presbyterian and Reformed, 1947.

———. *An Introduction to Systematic Theology*. Philipsburg, N.J.: Presbyterian and Reformed, 1978.

———. *The Case for Calvinism*. Philadelphia: Presbyterian and Reformed, 1963.

Vos, Geerhardus. "The Doctrine of the Covenant in Reformed Theology." In *Redemptive History and Biblical Interpretation: The Shorter Writings of Geerhardus Vos*. Ed. Richard B. Gaffin, Jr. Philipsburg, N.J.: Presbyterian and Reformed, 1980.

Warfield, B. B. "Calvin's Doctrine of the Trinity." In *Calvin and Augustine*. Philadelphia: Presbyterian and Reformed, 1956.

Wolff, Hans Walter. *Hosea: A Commentary on the Book of the Prophet Hosea*. Philadelphia: Fortress Press, 1978.

Wright, N. T. *The New Testament and the People of God*. Minneapolis: Fortress Press, 1992.

Scripture Index

Author Index

A

Aquinas, Thomas   23, 26, 34
Aristotle   56, 58, 68–70, 107
Arius   68, 121
Augustine   13, 14, 23–26,
    31–35, 42, 47, 51–55, 66–
    68, 77, 108, 109

B

Barth, Karl   14, 20, 21, 23,
    28, 32, 33, 45, 54, 59, 61,
    62, 84
Bavinck, Herman   47, 48, 52,
    54, 80, 84, 85, 95–98, 100
Berkhof, Hendrikus   28
Berkhof, Louis   15, 82
Bierma, Lyle D.   75, 101
Boethius   23
Bracken, Joseph   71

C

Calvin, John   14, 54, 59, 63,
    86, 100
Clark, Gordon   15, 56, 121,
    125, 126
Cloppenburg, Johannes   75
Cocceius, Johannes   75
Coleridge, Samuel Taylor   63

D

Dabney, R. L.   82, 83
Davis, Stephen   44, 45, 50, 51
DeMar, Gary   17
Dumbrell, William J.   79

E

Eichrodt, Walther   94
Erickson, Millard J.   44–46,
    48, 51, 57, 87, 106

F

Feinberg, Paul   66
Frame, John   125–28

G

Geisler, Norman   66
Grenz, Stanley   14, 87
Gunton, Colin   33–35, 55–
    57, 63, 106

H

Hasker, William   39
Heidegger, Martin   75
Henry, Carl F. H.   15, 105
Heppe, Heinrich   75, 76, 82
Heraclitus   56
Hilary   24, 68, 115–17